DEFENDER OF HUMAN RIGHTS

Carl Schurz

Born—March 2, 1829
Died—May 14, 1906

Carl Schurz early learned the price of idealism when, as a supporter of a democratic uprising, he was forced to flee the autocratic Germany of 1848. As a proud citizen of the United States, he could never rest while slavery existed, government offices were awarded as political favors rather than for merit, Indians were betrayed on the Western Plains, or while any type of injustice cast a shadow upon the country that he had made his own. As an ambassador, general, senator, cabinet member, crusading editor, and friend and advisor to presidents, his life offers vivid proof that devotion to principle, at whatever cost, is one of the highest forms of human courage.

Defender of Human Rights

CARL SCHURZ

by

James P. Terzian

Julian Messner New York

Published by Julian Messner
Division of Pocket Books, Inc.
8 West 40 Street, New York, N.Y. 10018

Printed in the United States of America
Library of Congress Catalog Card No. 65 22250

To Kathy and Zaza

DEFENDER OF HUMAN RIGHTS

Carl Schurz

1. A tall young figure, all arms and legs, bounded up the front steps of a small house and flung the door open.

"Mother! Mother, where are you!" The door slammed with a violence that shook the building to its foundation.

A woman's voice drifted down from the dimness of the second-floor landing. "Carl, is that you?" When she saw her son running up the stairs, taking the steps three at a time, her face went white. "Why aren't you in school?"

"Because there's no one there!" The boy's eyes fairly glowed behind heavy horn-rimmed glasses. "We've all marched out . . . students, professors–"

"Carl, what are you saying?"

His long arms beat the air. "I'm saying that if King Wilhelm won't support a popular government for all of Germany, then we will make him do it . . . and by force if necessary! We're mobilizing on the square now! Professor Kinkel himself is leading the militia! And I'm going with him!"

His excitement, however, could not hide the sharp thrill of fear that swept through his lean frame. Carl Schurz, barely nineteen in the summer of 1848, and just finishing his first year at the University of Bonn, was about to take part in an armed revolt against the trained armies of King Wilhelm of Prussia. And he hadn't so much as fired a shot in his entire life!

"No, Carl!" His mother threw herself at her son. "Wait for your father, at least!"

He pried her hands gently from his neck. "There's no time. We march in an hour. Oh, and I've been made an officer!" He snapped to exaggerated attention. "Lieutenant Carl Schurz of the Franconia Student Society of Bonn!"

For young Carl this was the start of a great adventure rising out of the many school debates and discussions on freedom and the popular vote. But for Frau Marianne Schurz, it was like living through an old dream. Years ago, she recalled, when she was still a girl, her older brother, Carl's uncle, had also marched against an earlier Prussian king in the revolution of 1815. That effort had failed; this attempt too, by the looks of it, would also fail. But she knew nothing could now hold back her only son. Ever since Carl had enrolled at the university a year ago, he had talked of the overthrow of the autocratic Wilhelm. Best to let him go, and pray for his safety.

Then she remembered something else. "Your uncle's sword! The one he used when he was your age! I must have it around here somewhere!" She hurried to the attic, Carl at her heels. After a frantic search among some old clothes, she dug out a long, slightly curved sword still attached to a military belt. "Take it, Carl! Use it with honor! It carried your uncle safely through the last political storm. God grant it bring you the same protection!"

The boy's eyes popped. A sword! Now he would be a real officer! He buckled the weapon around his narrow waist. "There, how do I look?"

Frau Schurz smiled bravely. Then, collapsing in his arms, she burst out into sobs.

The youthful band of students that gathered in front of

the broad marble steps of the university library presented a strange, almost comical appearance. Some were dressed in bits and pieces of old uniforms; some wore hiking shorts, others the rough clothes of farm boys. Many carried staves, pitchforks and axes as weapons; a dozen or so proudly bore rusty muskets on their shoulders. But there was one common insignia in this patchwork pattern: the red, black and gold armband of the Franconia Society, the local university organization that had taken for its slogan the French revolutionary call of "Liberty, Equality, Fraternity!"

The students shouted this cry over and over again as the sun beat down on their flushed, excited faces. Finally a deep-chested, broad-shouldered man, wearing a flowing red cape and a wide-brimmed hat, climbed the topmost step of the library. The hubbub died down almost at once.

Two men, standing apart from the swarms of townspeople that had gathered around the university square, began whispering to one another. Neither took his eyes off the figure in the red cape. "So that's the leader, is it?" one of them said.

"Yes, Herr Captain. Professor Gottfried Kinkel himself. The professor-patriot, they call him. A teacher of history and rhetoric."

"A teacher of treason!" The man addressed as Captain shifted his gaze. "And that tall young fellow, the one with the sword dangling from his side. Seems pretty close to Kinkel, yes?"

"Oh, he is, Captain! Master and pupil from what I hear. His name is Carl Schurz."

"Those are the two we're after then. Put their names on the list, Sergeant. Kinkel, number one. Schurz, number two."

Agents of King Wilhelm, these two men had been sent down from Frankfurt to spy out the strategy of the student army. This they were able to do with no trouble whatever.

All week long there had been talk of open revolt. In the event the king failed to heed the demands of the assembly —and that time was now—the Bonn students would board the ferry to Rostatt, a fort some one hundred miles to the southeast along the Rhine River, capture it and hand it over to the large revolutionary force marching down from Frankfurt, seat of the Prussian government. With so many Germans, including large segments of the army itself, dissatisfied with the imperious Wilhelm, the revolt couldn't help but succeed. It was as simple as that, and no secret about the plan.

Gottfried Kinkel, as leader of the revolutionary group, now underlined the urgency of the cause. "Citizens and patriots—" he began, and the crowd let out another loud cheer. Standing at his side, Carl Schurz bristled with pride. How splendid to be a part of history, instead of just reading about it!

"My fellow liberators," the professor continued, "we have nothing to hide from the king, least of all our aspirations! And he has nothing to fear from us. We are first of all Germans, not traitors; free men, not slaves. Our hope is the hope for all Prussia, for all Germany—a constitutional government based on the popular vote. That is our goal and that will be our victory!"

A tremendous roar greeted these words. Forgetting his dignity as an officer, Carl threw his hat in the air, then escorted his leader down the steps. A small cannon boomed, a band struck up a march, and the youthful army, perhaps three hundred in all, began to file out of the square. Women and children ran alongside, throwing kisses and flowers. Older men shouted hoarse words of encouragement. The band tooted on, marching behind. It too, like the ragtag army, was out of step.

Carl heard the cheers only dimly. Dust choked his throat, stung his eyes. He had difficulty breathing. For just one moment he felt a powerful urge to quit this wild adventure and return home to his books, his family and his music. But only for a moment. Most of his friends were here with him, in the ranks. Their goal, perhaps only a military campaign away, had been the dream of their young lives: the unity and political freedom of Germany.

Carl Schurz was keenly disappointed at the ease with which Rostatt was captured the following morning. Not even a shot had been fired as the rebels marched up to the gates and demanded that Rostatt surrender to the forces of the provisional German Republic. The fort's only soldier, a frightened little sergeant (not even an officer, Carl thought, with some disgust) had simply handed over the keys to the garrison. The student-soldiers were now strutting about the compound, congratulating themselves. So this is war, they thought. More like child's play!

Just then a cannon boomed in the distance. Carl looked up in time to see a gray puff of smoke rising ominously against the blue sky. A moment later, a sentry screamed down an alarm from the lookout tower. "From the forest! We're being fired on from the forest!"

"Bolt the gates!" Commander Kinkel turned to Carl. "Lieutenant, secure the entry!"

But the Rostatt gates, as if anticipating his command, seemed to swing shut of their own accord, but not before the grinning sergeant skipped past the ponderous, iron-laced doors to his freedom.

Carl raced up the high walls of the fort. What he saw on the outside almost made his heart turn over. "The king's soldiers!" he called down. "They're pouring out of the woods, bolting the gates! Professor, we're in a trap . . . surrounded on all sides!"

Not only surrounded, but as a quick search of the fort later revealed, the rebel army was without guns and ammunition. Or even food and water. "The place," Carl concluded grimly, "is as bare as Mother Hubbard's cupboard."

"Then we'll fight with sticks and stones, drink rain water and live off our rations until the revolutionary army from Frankfurt comes to our rescue." Commander Kinkel looked over his suddenly subdued forces. "Who's with me?"

They all were with him, despite the sudden turn of events. Carl led the determined cheers that answered their leader's challenge. This was more like it! A siege . . . the siege of Rostatt! War, finally, had joined the cause of freedom!

Twenty-three days later, hunger, thirst and illness had dulled the fine edge of revolution.

"It's no use," Gottfried Kinkel finally announced to his corps of student officers on the evening of the twenty-third day. "We've been outmaneuvered."

"But, sir! What about the supporting army from Frankfurt?" Carl Schurz gripped the hilt of his sword, symbol of his youthful defiance. "Maybe they're marching to save us . . . right now!"

The haggard-looking professor, wearing his cloak against an approaching storm, pulled a document from under its folds. "This came an hour ago." He unfolded the paper which bore the official seal of the king. "It's from the commander of the besieging forces." He began to read the message. It was brief and to the point: the Frankfurt rebels, it stated, had been intercepted and scattered, their leaders captured. In view of the hopeless situation, and in an effort to avoid bloodshed, it continued, the king had decreed military pardon and safe conduct home for the Bonn rebels if they surrendered within twenty-four hours. Otherwise, Rostatt would be attacked. "It will be their guns against our stones," Kinkel warned as the first rumble of distant thunder echoed in the command room. "For the safety of our company I recommend surrender on enemy terms."

Carl reached for his sword automatically. To surrender now would mean handing over his uncle's weapon to the enemy! Use it with honor, his mother had said. What honor was there in giving up without a fight?

The professor, as usual, seemed to read his mind. "We accept defeat now in order to prepare for victory next time. If all rebels gave up with their first loss, freedom would have few friends. Now, shall we prepare for morning?"

Carl agreed reluctantly, after which Kinkel delegated responsibilities for the surrender. It suddenly occurred to the young lieutenant that not once had his name been mentioned. With some annoyance he asked if he had been forgotten.

"Hardly, Carl," the professor replied. "You are to be the star attraction tomorrow. You and the Donath brothers"—he motioned to Emil and Ludwig Donath, twin brothers who were also rebel aides—"will help carry on the revolution . . . *in absentia.*"

Kinkel quickly explained. "The king's pardon does not include either of us, Carl. On the contrary, it is specific that you and I will be placed under arrest for our part in leading this revolt. But there's no use both of us going to prison. So I've drawn up a plan for your escape, Carl—no, no, I insist! It *must* be you! If I don't give myself up tomorrow, they'll throw the whole company into irons. And that I will not allow."

"But both our names are on that document!" Carl protested. "What if *I* don't show up?"

Kinkel had an answer for that, too. "They don't know for certain that you *are* with us. Sure, you were seen on the way to Rostatt, but that's about all. I will explain that on the march to the ferry, back in Bonn, you turned your ankle and fell by the wayside and eventually made your way to France. In other words, you were never part of the besieged company."

"But escape . . . how? You said yourself—" Another roll of thunder, closer this time, warned of the approaching storm.

The weary professor let out a sigh. "We haven't much time. Now listen closely. . . ."

His plan was simple. Several days before, while exploring the fort with the Donath brothers, Kinkel had stumbled on a hidden underground sewer that led to an outside gulch which, in turn, emptied into the nearby Rhine River. The crude tunnel was about a mile in length. "The only catch is, enemy guards have been posted at the other end of the sewer."

"Then how can we—"

"I'm coming to that. After the surrender tomorrow morning our troops will probably be marched to the ferry for the trip back home. Now that road, according to the Donath brothers, who come from this area, passes near where the sewer guards are stationed. Emil and Ludwig say they know the countryside as well as their books. Perhaps even better," Kinkel added with a smile, "which is why I asked them to volunteer for this assignment!"

At two o'clock that night, at the peak of a booming thunderstorm, Carl, the Donath twins and Kinkel gathered at the mouth of the tunnel. "Now remember," the latter warned, "you are to make no move until we start the diversionary action. You will first hear a scream, then my voice. Our little charade should take place an hour or two after sunrise, depending on how soon we are escorted to the ferry."

Carl nodded. Desperate situations called for desperate measures. From now on it would be a matter of timing, and courage. He wondered if he was up to the challenge. He looked at the dark sky, as if for an answer. Rain pelted his drawn face, smeared his glasses, but he was aware only of Kinkel's parting words.

". . . with one of us free, Carl," he was saying, "the chances of the other rotting in prison are cut by half. Godspeed, my boy!"

Carl gripped his sword and plunged into the gloom of the underground passageway, his free hand tugging at the rope which kept him in communication with Emil and Ludwig, who were some ten feet in front of him.

The half-finished sewer was high enough for the average man to walk through without bending over, but the lanky young Schurz—he was now two inches over six feet—had to crouch painfully in order to protect his head against the rocky overhead. The wet and slippery ground made progress doubly difficult, and of course a light was out of the question. That mile of slimy, Stygian darkness would have to be negotiated by hand and foot, by courage and instinct.

The eerie blackness, the uncertainty of the outcome, filled Carl with fear. A knee-high pool of water soaked him as he stumbled and fell. The scrambling of rats unnerved him. Once he pitched forward into a puddle of mud. But he held on to the rope; a reassuring tug told him the twins were still moving forward. This was no time to turn tail. What was it

Kinkel had said just before the parting? ". . . with one of us free . . . the chances of the other rotting in prison are cut by half."

Did the professor mean by that someday, he, Carl Schurz, would help *him* escape? Carl swore he would, provided he himself got out of this mess!

After what seemed like an endless night underground, he thought he saw something up ahead less black than the surrounding darkness. A tug of the rope brought one of the twins back with news that the other end of the tunnel was indeed in sight. Carl decided it was now time for him to take the lead, when danger was greatest. "From here on," he warned, "not a sound!" A slip, a dislodged stone, a grunt of pain, the slightest accident could give them away to whoever might be standing guard at the other end of the sewer. And there was someone out there, no question about it! Carl heard a murmur of voices, a clank of metal on metal; a hidden flame threw weird shadows halfway into their hiding place.

The three youths slowed to a crawl, a dangerous, oozing, muddy crawl, until they were no more than fifteen yards from that yawning patch of gray. Motioning to the twins to lie low, Carl edged forward on his hands and knees, then froze. There, in the clearing ahead, he saw two soldiers huddling over a campfire and brewing a pot of coffee!

He would have given anything for a hot cup of coffee then, perhaps even his freedom. But he shook off the temptation; he was, after all, the senior officer of the escape party. With the tantalizing aroma of freshly brewed coffee still in his nostrils, he crawled back and ordered a watch until daybreak.

"I'll take the first hour," he whispered, scooping up a handful of muddy water to help him keep awake. The twins nodded, curled up against each other, and fell into a damp, deep sleep.

The slowly lightening eastern sky revived the weary Carl. When the early morning sun began to filter through the dripping trees—the rain had stopped—he woke his companions. *Only a little longer,* he motioned in dumb show, forming the words with lips numbed from fatigue. The twins nodded and ducked back into the shadows.

That hour was the longest in the boy's young life. Where were Kinkel's forces? Had something gone wrong, he wondered? Perhaps the troops had taken another route, or maybe the enemy had gone back on its word or—

Then he heard them, the welcome, far-off sounds of shuffling feet and distant voices. The sentries heard, too. "Here they come," one soldier said to the other. "They've finally surrendered, think of that! Twenty-three days . . . I wouldn't have given them that many hours!"

Sounds drifted in from the road beyond, an occasional youthful laugh or a man's harsher command to "stay in line and keep to the road, you!" Carl peered past the dense underbrush. He saw nothing of the advancing column. But a large group of marchers *was* coming closer, no question about that!

A moment later an anguished scream curdled his insides. The sentries jumped to the alert as shouts of "Come back! Come back, you fool!" reached them. Kinkel's voice! The diversionary action was under way!

Suddenly a wild figure, eyes rolling, mouth agape, arms flailing, crashed into the clearing and pitched forward to his knees. Carl recognized him at once as Hans Kummel, a fellow student who frequently starred in university dramatics. What a performance, he thought, watching flecks of foam spray from Hans' lips!

The two army sentries, rifles at the ready, rushed forward. In another moment, other soldiers, followed by a mob of students, crashed into the clearing, surrounding the stricken boy. They formed a convenient screen between the sentries and the mouth of the tunnel.

That was all the advantage Carl needed. Shoving the twins before him, he slipped out of his hiding place, ducked into the dense underbrush and threw himself into a deep gully, and never mind the bruises! They were out of their dank trap and on the way to freedom! The last thing Carl heard was Gottfried Kinkel's voice murmuring something about "the poor lad, he always was subject to epileptic fits. . . ."

The three escapees now scurried along the gully, in the direction of the river. There they remained in hiding for the rest of the long day while hunger, flies and mosquitoes plagued them. With the sun down and darkness descending, Emil Donath scrambled out of the gulch. "It's safe now," he whispered. "I know where I can get some help." He returned an hour later accompanied by an old peasant.

"He'll row you across the river to France, Carl. He has a rowboat not far from here. We've promised him a reward after he lands you on the other side."

"But you and your brother . . . Aren't you coming along?"

"We're wanted by no one but our families. We will now go home and send word to Kinkel that you made it. We'll also tell your parents."

They parted warmly, the twins taking the road to town, Carl and the peasant heading for the river.

Just before boarding the leaky skiff the old man put a twisted hand on the boy's arm. "A young rebel, wanted by the police, is that it?" He grinned a toothless smile. "I'm taking an awful chance, I am. It must be worth something, rowing you to freedom, eh?"

"But my friends will pay you! I haven't a *pfennig!*"

The old peasant cracked his gums again. "Who said anything about money?" His eyes fell on the sword strapped around Carl's waist. "That weapon would make a real fine souvenir, I'd say. Something to tell my grandchildren about the siege of Rostatt, and the young man who *almost* made it to France!"

Carl gulped, reaching for his belt buckle. Later, halfway across the river to France and freedom, it suddenly occurred to him that he was now a refugee, a man without a friend, without a sword and without a country.

2.

Carl Schurz was born on March 2, 1829, on a royal estate near Liblar, Germany, a village nestled in the rolling Rhine Valley.

His mother, Marianne, a simple, hard-working woman, was in charge of servants' quarters in the castle of Count Wolf Metternich, a nobleman serving the Prussian king. His father was the local schoolteacher; Christian Schurz was a kind, gentle man devoted to books and music.

Circumstances of birth thus placed the boy squarely between the pomp of aristocracy on one side and the poverty of the Count's bonded peasants on the other. Even at a very early age he asked why fine ladies and gentlemen of the court spent most of their time at play while peasants had to work long hours in the fields and barns belonging to the Count.

"Someday, when you read history, my son," his father told him, "you'll learn that things in this world aren't always the way you'd like them to be." Nevertheless, seeing for himself how the rich lived off the poor made a deep impression on young Schurz, one that was to set the direction of his later years.

Schoolmaster Schurz also passed on to Carl a paternal passion for music and literature. He encouraged him to read well beyond his years, and from his meager teacher's salary, bought a battered old piano and gave him lessons. When the boy showed an aptitude for the instrument, he arranged for private instruction with the local *Kapellmeister,* a director of music. In later years, the piano became one of Carl's most enduring interests.

The boy was also fond of the outdoors. Walking six miles each way to the *gymnasium* in Cologne—the equivalent of our combined junior-senior high school—he would ramble along the Rhine tributaries, hunting for frogs or lizards or picking wild flowers. Or on warm days, he might stretch out on the riverbank and memorize Greek and Latin verses, required reading in those days even for boys of ten or twelve.

During the bitter German winters, however, Carl boarded out in Cologne with friends, going home only for the Christmas and Easter holidays. His own family, meantime, had been enlarged to include a younger brother and two sisters.

But then misfortune struck. Herbert, the brother, never very strong, died of pneumonia. Several years later, Christian Schurz was thrown into prison for failure to pay his debts. This forced Carl to drop out of school during his last year in the *gymnasium* in order to help his family.

Only seventeen and practically the head of a household! Yet the lanky young Schurz, nearly six feet tall and as thin as a birch, seemed to thrive on adversity. After borrowing money from a sympathetic uncle, he paid most of his father's debts, then, with a passionate plea, convinced the local judge to release the elder Schurz from jail.

"Watch that boy," the magistrate predicted. "He has a gift of oratory with which he can twist the devil's tail."

With family affairs settled, Carl made an important decision. Since he was so fond of history—he had won a number of prizes in that subject before dropping out of school—he would continue his education and perhaps become a professor or even a statesman. "But I've missed my last year at the *gymnasium,* Father. If I go back now I'll fall a year behind my schoolmates. Will you help me study on my own so I can enter the university with my class?"

For the next six months father and son poured over their texts. Then, in preparation for Carl's college days, the Schurz family moved to Bonn, site of the famous German university. And there, with mounting apprehension, they sat helplessly by as he underwent the rigors of special examinations, made doubly difficult in order to discourage "wild card" students like Carl from enrolling.

On a bright sunny morning in September, 1847, a nervous young man found himself behind a large oak desk forever marked by a hundred student carvings, some dating back to 1784 when the University of Bonn was founded. As was the custom in those days, special examinations were given in private; Carl was the only one in the room except for the proctor, a solemn heavy-set man who towered over the quaking candidate.

"You are Carl Schurz?" he heard the proctor say. The boy nodded.

"I am Professor Gottfried Kinkel, doctor of history and rhetoric. I will examine you in these subjects as well as Latin, Greek, mathematics and science. I am permitted to answer no questions except to tell you the time of day . . . or night. On the other hand, I may ask *you* any question on any subject, which you must answer orally and to my entire satisfaction. This in addition to the written requirements. Is that understood?"

The boy nodded stiffly, swallowing hard.

"Very well, you may begin." Professor Kinkel, one of the most brilliant scholars at Bonn in spite of his comparative youth—he was still in his middle thirties at the time—reached for a stack of papers. "Your first requirement is to write the complete history of modern Germany. I advise you to answer most completely, Schurz. That subject happens to be a specialty of mine."

There is no telling where the story of Carl Schurz would have led had it not been for that particular question. German history was Carl's favorite subject. He was also an avid student of political freedom. In writing about events in his native country, the boy drew frequent comparisons with the French and American revolutions; the Declaration of Independence he had committed to memory (in German, of course), and he could recite the Bill of Rights as well as his own name.

What we call Germany today, both East and West, was in the 1840's a loose group of independent states, each governed by royalty. Some states were small and insignificant. Others were larger, more powerful. But nearly all bickered among themselves over borders and tariffs, throwing their armies and allegiances to whichever ruling prince promised greater rewards. In this constant struggle, the people themselves, especially the peasants, seldom enjoyed political and social freedom. To many liberals, the first step necessary to achieve these ends was the consolidation of all these separate state governments into one strong federal union.

The largest and most powerful German state then was Prussia, ruled by Frederick Wilhelm IV, an autocrat who promised much in the way of reform but delivered little. It was he, more than anyone else, who blocked federation. And it was Wilhelm against whom Carl now aimed his political shafts.

He could not have chosen a better target. Gottfried Kinkel, known throughout Bonn as the "professor-patriot," was himself the king's severest critic and a great champion of the popular vote. When he picked up Carl's paper that morning, fully expecting another schoolboy recitation of dry statistics,

Kinkel opened his eyes in surprise. What he read were words on fire, also an unerring organization of fact and logic. True, the lad's responses were somewhat impetuous, perhaps a bit idealistic. But the seeds of freedom were there!

The proctor gave the boy a long and searching look. The university—no, Germany itself—had need of such a mind!

Happily for Carl, he passed all his other examinations with good grades, though he might have made a stronger showing in mathematics and science. But Professor Kinkel made a personal appearance before the board of examiners —an event rare in itself—and used all his persuasive powers in behalf of the applicant, calling Schurz a candidate "uniquely qualified and exceptionally gifted."

The examiners looked at one another gravely. They knew Gottfried Kinkel to be a man of the highest principle and unquestioned scholarship. If he was willing to accept the boy, could they do anything less?

The year that followed was one of the happiest in the young man's life. Throwing himself into his university studies, Carl took to academic life with vigor and enthusiasm. He read Homer, Plato and Goethe; Shakespeare was his constant companion. He immersed himself in the writings of Martin Luther and read and reread the French philosophers, especially Voltaire.

Carl also enjoyed the give-and-take of argument; his agile mind soon made him one of the better debaters at the university. Much to his delight, he was invited to join the Franconia Society, the student political group led by Gottfried Kinkel himself.

A strong master-pupil relationship quickly developed between the brilliant Kinkel and the knowledge-hungry Schurz. Carl attended many meetings at which the "professor-patriot" spoke. Once he accompanied Kinkel to Frankfurt where the newly formed Prussian constitutional assembly, grudgingly convened by the king, tried to make its feelings known to the crown. But it had little success. Wilhelm had placed too many palace advisers between himself and his subjects for popular sentiment ever to reach him.

Carl regaled his family with accounts of his student activities. He talked of ". . . mass meetings to protest the king's refusal to heed the assembly . . ." or ". . . in this debate I'm speaking for the popular vote as against rule by edict. . . ."

And so the months flew by. In the spring of 1848, Carl received an honor seldom given first-year students—he was made an officer of the Franconia Society. After his installation, Professor Kinkel told him that "if ever we take action against the king, I want you at my side."

"Gladly, sir!" He had no idea then that this commitment, freely given, would one day bring him into the fateful trap at Rostatt, and later send him to France and Switzerland as a revolutionary and enemy of the king.

In the early spring of 1849, a tall young man paced restlessly in a garret in the city of Zurich, Switzerland. From time to time he pulled back the curtains of the room's single window to peer out at the darkening streets below. Obviously, he was waiting for someone or something.

Eight months since the escape from Rostatt had wrought a number of changes in Carl Schurz's appearance. He had, if anything, grown thinner, which accentuated his height. He seemed older, more subdued; in brief, his months of exile had changed him from a schoolboy to a man.

He had been brought to Switzerland by Kinkel's friends, for they knew that if anyone could help Kinkel escape it would be this gangling young man with a mission. The professor, meanwhile, had been tried and sentenced to life imprisonment and placed in the fortress-jail of Spandau, a suburb of Berlin.

Ever since coming to Zurich, Carl had been working on a plan to free Kinkel. He had finally decided on a bold scheme, one that would require money, outside help and daring. Kinkel's friends willingly supplied the first two; the third was up to Schurz himself.

First, the young exile grew a moustache in order to look older; he changed from heavy horn-rimmed glasses to light, silver-rimmed spectacles. Then he found another refugee, a German like himself, who had spent some time in Spandau as a prisoner. From him he learned all about the notorious political prison, its layout, schedule, even the names of the guards. He was told to look up a certain Waldemar Brume, a jailer who was fond of bribes and beer. Finally, he obtained a passport from a former schoolmate, Abraham Jacobi, now a medical student in Zurich. "Of course you can borrow my passport," Jacobi had said. "I'd gladly sacrifice it for Kinkel's freedom. Seems hardly enough, though, since you're putting your life in danger." It was the medical student for whom Carl was now waiting so restlessly in the garret.

Jacobi arrived shortly after dark bringing good news. "We have raised enough money for you to stay in Berlin for at least a month. We have also arranged passage for the professor, his family and you aboard a schooner which leaves the port of Warnemunde [on the northern coast of Germany] bound for England. It sails promptly at sunrise every other Saturday. You'll find the schedule in here." He tapped a medical kit. "And do you remember the Donath twins? They are now in Berlin, working as coachmen. They know the inn where you'll be staying. But, Carl, tell me this. How the devil do you expect to get Kinkel out of prison?"

"First things first." Carl tucked the money into his wallet along with his passport. "You say I've got at least a month in Berlin? Well, if I can't figure out an escape by then, I deserve to be thrown into prison along with Kinkel!" Then he wrapped himself in Jacobi's dark cloak, put on his top hat and picked up the medical kit, all trademarks of the European doctor. "How do I look, Abraham?"

Jacobi smiled in satisfaction. "Like a real sawbones! Here, let me show you how to use this stethoscope in case anyone asks for treatment. In which case you keep your mouth shut, nod gravely and charge him a hundred marks. Well, that's it, Carl. Good-bye, old friend. *Auf wiedersehn!*"

Carl clasped Jacobi's hand. "Till we meet again. I wonder when that will be? Or *if* . . . ?"

"Enough, enough! You'll have me in tears. And remember, from this minute on, you're *Herr Doktor!*"

Carl had no difficulty either at the border or on the long train ride to Berlin. He was, as a matter of fact, accorded extreme courtesy. It was "Good morning, *Herr Doktor,*" or "Pleasant journey, *mein Herr.*" Neither did he have difficulty renting a room in the small inn not far from the imposing prison at Spandau picked out for him by his friends in Switzerland.

That night he had a joyful reunion with Emil and Ludwig Donath. The twins, dressed as coachmen, drove Carl for a visit with Mrs. Kinkel who, with her two daughters, had rented an apartment in Spandau in order to be close to her husband. They also took him to the Three Falcons, a tavern the prison guards frequented. "Take your meals here," Emil advised. "Let it be known that you're a student on vacation and that you've plenty of money to spend. I guarantee those guards will sniff the bait soon enough."

Emil was right. The Spandau jailers came to the Three

Falcons that very night, complaining loudly of long hours and short pay. It was an easy matter for Carl to introduce himself; he simply offered to pay for their food and drinks. The surprised guards responded by inviting him to sit at their table and toast King Wilhelm's health. This he did with a straight face.

It was then that he first heard the name "Brume." The fellow thus addressed by his fellow guards was a short, unshaven individual with rheumy eyes and a fawning manner. Remembering that this man had been mentioned as his best contact in Spandau, Carl began to cultivate his friendship, distasteful as it was. Brume, for his part, fairly beamed at the honor being paid him. From then on he made it a point to drop in at the Three Falcons for a glass or two with the youthful visitor from Zurich.

By the end of the week Carl was quite sure he had the guard's friendship. "Tell me, Brume," he began one evening after buying him his dinner, "do you know of a certain prisoner named Kinkel? Gottfried Kinkel?"

Brume opened his watery eyes wide. "Oho, do I *not* know him, *Herr Doktor!* He's a prize one, he is!" He bent over confidentially. "They say he's in for treason, that's what!" Then he drew off suspiciously. "Why do you ask?"

His host remained disinterested. "Nothing much. I once treated him for a lung condition in Switzerland. When his wife learned I was here on holiday she begged me to see him." He dropped a small bag of coins on the table. "She's very worried about his condition. However"—he reached for the money with a sigh—"if such a thing is impossible. . . ."

The guard measured the bait. "Who said impossible, eh?" The money bag disappeared into his jacket.

Brume proved to be as clever as he was greedy. Two days

later, after another bribe for the floor warden, he led his guest up the winding stone steps of the prison to a cell high in the tower. Carl Schurz tagged along, conspicuously carrying his black medical bag. At last Brume stopped in front of a barred door at the end of the corridor. "There's your man, *Herr Doktor.* But I'll have to go in with you. Regulations, you know."

The former student gasped at the sight of his professor. Gottfried Kinkel lay motionless on a narrow cot; he had lost weight and his once black hair had turned nearly white. Sunken eyes stared back without recognition.

"Good morning," Carl began cheerfully, as a physician might. "Remember me from the clinic in Zurich, Professor? How are the lungs? Any better?"

Kinkel almost jumped at the sound of that familiar voice. However, he quickly recovered, threw his unexpected visitor a sly wink, then began to cough so violently that for a moment Carl was fearful that his friend had, indeed, contracted a terrible illness. But a reassuring nod during the examination told him that the patient was perfectly sound and alert.

Carl knew now he had to battle for time. It would take something more than money to get Kinkel out of prison. "Worse than I thought," he announced gravely as he snapped the medical kit shut. "Brume, do you suppose you can arrange for another pass later in the week?" He drew a bank note from his pocket.

The guard rubbed his hands. "Highly irregular, *Herr Doktor,* but I'll see what can be done."

From then on, Carl was a frequent visitor to Kinkel's cell. Because of his generosity, he soon became as popular with the guards as the Spandau paymaster. But by the end of the month, money and time were both in danger of running out. He checked his calendar. The ship for England was scheduled to sail the next Saturday morning from Warnemunde. It was imperative to get the professor out of prison before then.

A plan had been drawn up days in advance. Carl now decided to put it into operation. First, he instructed the Donath twins to prepare the carriage for a long night journey to the seaport. Then he told Kinkel's wife to be ready to flee with her two young children shortly after midnight. And finally he prepared his medical bag, placing in it a coil of stout rope, a short crowbar and a small bottle of colored liquid. He checked its label to make certain the writing on it was legible.

The following afternoon he told a sorrowful Brume that this would be his last visit. The guard was genuinely distressed at the thought of losing his extra fees.

Later, in the cell, the "doctor" announced that his patient was well on the road to recovery. "But just in case you start coughing again, Professor, I've brought you some medicine. May I, Brume?" Carl waved the medicine toward Kinkel with one hand; the other held a large bank note.

"Highly irregular," the guard smiled. "But if it's for the prisoner's health—"

"Oh, but it is!" Carl assured him, then handed the bottle to Kinkel. "Read the directions carefully, Professor. Do you understand them?"

Kinkel glanced down at the label on the bottle. The directions were written in Latin. *Your next dose is in my medical bag,* he read to himself. *Open it as soon as I leave, then wait for the call of the midnight owl.* His eyes betrayed no emotion. "I understand, *Herr Doktor*. I will take my medication as instructed."

Carl nodded gravely, trying hard to suppress his excitement. The final consultation had come off without a hitch.

"Good-bye, Professor. And stay well." The iron door clanged shut as he and the guard left the cell.

It was only after they reached the bottom of the winding stone steps that Brume sounded the alarm. *"Herr Doktor!"*

Carl turned, stalling for time. "Yes . . . ?"

"Your bag, sir! You must have left it upstairs!"

"What?" He seemed befuddled. "Oh, yes! How stupid of me!" He began the slow ascent up the stairway, muttering something about his forgetfulness. When Brume finally retrieved the kit, Carl's heart pounded with triumph. The bag was far lighter than it had been only minutes before!

An hour after midnight, as all of Spandau lay silent under a moonless night, a shuttered carriage drove into the street bordering the prison. The rubber-rimmed wheels made no sound. Even the horses' hoofs were muffled, making a soft "whap-whap" as the carriage came to a stop on the wet cobblestones. A moment later a tall thin figure, dressed in a flowing cloak, stepped out and looked high up at the walls of the prison, toward the tower. He let out a low whistle, like the haunting hoot of an owl.

At that signal one end of a rope came hurtling out of the darkness. "Let it be long enough," Carl prayed. It was; he grabbed its lower end. "And strong enough."

As if in answer, the head and shoulders of a man squeezed through the twisted bars of a window high up on the Spandau walls. Carl held his breath as Gottfried Kinkel let himself down hand over hand until his feet touched the street.

They scrambled into the carriage, Kinkel first, huffing and puffing at the exertion, Carl right behind him. Ten minutes later the coach rolled up in front of a small house. A woman and two children, each carrying bundles, ran down a short flight of steps and climbed into the waiting vehicle.

Carl Schurz waited a moment for Professor Kinkel to embrace his wife. Then he stuck his head out of the window. "To the sea, Emil!" he whispered urgently to the driver. "The ship sails from Warnemunde at sunrise!"

That mad dash to the sea, and the subsequent flight to England aboard the schooner, made Carl Schurz a celebrity in the German colony of London. He found himself the center of attention wherever he went, introduced to one and all by a grateful Kinkel as "my deliverer and rescuer."

Carl blushed at the attention rained on him, impressed once more by the esteem in which his former professor was held. This esteem, moreover, had its practical side, especially to a young man with little money. His most pressing need, at the moment, was a job.

"We must see to that at once," Kinkel agreed when Carl told him that he could hardly continue to exist on the dinners given in his honor by appreciative German refugees.

He was offered a post as correspondent for a German paper published in England by one of Kinkel's friends. Carl accepted gladly, since it involved traveling to Paris, Geneva and Brussels. But he was careful not to set foot anywhere in Germany, where he was still a wanted man. In fact, his newfound freedom was somewhat diminished by reports from Bonn that his mother and father were constantly harassed by King Wilhelm's secret police.

"They question us constantly," his father wrote in a letter smuggled out of Germany. "We are even roused out of bed in the middle of the night. But, of course, we tell the police nothing, only that you are not at home. Perhaps, by making our lives uncomfortable here, they hope to draw you back to Germany. Whatever you do, dear Carl, do not make the mistake of returning. Your rescue of Kinkel has given His Majesty's security forces a severe jolt, one they would dearly like to pay back by putting you on the end of a hangman's noose. In the meantime, we are well and send you our prayers and love. . . ."

It was a restless period for young Schurz. During the next three years he traveled about the Continent, sending back accounts of German refugees for his London-based paper. Each time he reported on a scholar or scientist who had fled Wilhelm's wrath, he got a measure of satisfaction. But only a measure. For he was still a man without a country, without a mission, really. Carl Schurz, at twenty-three, would much have preferred to be in the midst of the struggle for liberty than on the outside looking in.

He said as much one evening to a young lady sitting next to him at a London dinner party. She was introduced to him as Margarethe Mayer, the daughter of a well-known German merchant who had also taken refuge in England. "All people do nowadays is talk, talk, talk," Carl complained. "Or, like myself, they write about political oppression. No one ever seems to take action!"

Margarethe Mayer smiled behind her fan. "Another mad dash to the sea, Herr Schurz?"

Carl grinned. "There it is again, that confounded jailbreak. I wish people would be as eager to question me about the advantages of the secret ballot or the right to petition government!"

"Are those things important to you—?"

"But they are!"

"Then I will be happy to hear what you have to say about the secret ballot and the right to . . . to . . ."

"To petition government! Would you really like me to talk about them, Fraulein Mayer?"

They spent many evenings together after that. It wasn't altogether to the young man's discredit that he soon found himself discoursing on art and music and romantic literature to the young lady who, in his own words, "had a fine stature, a curly head of hair and large, truthful eyes."

After a brief courtship, Carl Schurz, formerly of Liblar, was married on July 6, 1852, to Margarethe Mayer, formerly of Hamburg, in the parish church of Marylebone, London.

For their honeymoon, he suggested a trip to America.

"But why just a honeymoon?" his bride exclaimed. "After all you've said about political freedom, dear Carl, I think we should plan to live there . . . for good!"

3.

Carl and Margarethe Schurz landed in New York on September 17, 1852. Within twenty-four hours they regretted ever having come to the New World. They knew few people in the big city; they were lonely and depressed. The bustle and noise of the metropolis only made their isolation more acute. After a gloomy week of tramping the streets and looking for work, Carl was ready to book passage back to London on the next ship.

He was sitting on a park bench in Union Square Park one day, seriously thinking of such a move, when a shadow fell across his face. He looked up to see a young man staring down at him. Carl shifted his seat. This was no time to be talking to strangers, or rather, *trying* to talk to them. He knew very little English while no one, it seemed, knew German at all, at least in this part of the city.

The shadow, however, persisted. Carl moved to the edge of the bench, only to have the young man move along with him.

"Bitte," the stranger began, speaking a phrase in German. "But aren't you—?"

Carl almost fell off the bench. That voice! "Jacobi!" he exclaimed.

"Schurz!" the other cried.

They fell into each other's arms. They danced and pounded each other and tried to tell their stories all at once.

Finally they relaxed over a cup of coffee at a nearby restaurant.

Jacobi told his story quickly. After completing his basic medical studies in Switzerland, he had come to America where he hoped to qualify for his degree and settle down to practice. "That will take, oh, another two or three years. Now, how about you?"

Carl was less ecstatic. Jacobi guessed the reason—homesickness. He therefore advised him to move to Philadelphia. "I have friends there, refugees like yourself, many from the revolution. They'll help you get started. I tell you, Carl, once you get to know America and what it promises, you'll forget all about going back. Now, why don't you take me home and introduce me to your bride?"

A few days later, the young couple moved to Philadelphia where they rented a modest cottage in a suburb called Germantown, settled by immigrants from the old country. As Jacobi had indicated, life was much more agreeable there. After several months, the newlyweds were joined by Carl's family, who were finally allowed to leave Germany, probably on the assumption that the fewer Schurzes remaining in the fatherland, the better for the government of King Wilhelm.

He first heard the word "greenhorn"—a name for immigrants who had not yet adjusted to American ways—during those early days. He sensed a note of derision in it. "Then I will not be a greenhorn for long," he resolved. With Carl, to resolve was to act.

Language was his chief problem. In London and throughout Europe, he had used German almost exclusively, since most of his contacts were refugees. The mother tongue, unfortunately for him, was also the language of his new community. He soon realized that he had to read, speak and write English fluently or remain shut up in Germantown.

He began by reading third- and fourth-grade textbooks, then worked his way up to the higher grades. He haunted the local library. His first requests for reading matter were spoken with a mixture of bad English and excellent German. A sympathetic librarian tried to help him by speaking bad German and excellent English.

Carl practically lived with a bilingual dictionary, pronouncing the English words aloud until they sounded as "American as in the streets I hear," he told Margarethe. Try as he might, however, he continued to have difficulty avoiding the inverted sentence structure peculiar to German grammar.

He also read novels, pamphlets, handbills, history books, anything published in English. He pored over newspapers, page by page. Nothing escaped his attention; he even read the advertisements. Soon he was the best-informed man in Germantown. "You want to know something?" one neighbor said to another. "About what President Pierce thinks or what the Secretary of State has to say or the price of liverwurst? Then go ask Carl Schurz. He knows everything."

Within six months he could speak English as well as his native tongue, though with a marked accent. He tried to overcome this by reciting Shakespeare out loud, even in the streets, much to the astonishment of passersby. The rolling cadences of the Bard's soliloquies gave his speech a distinct poetic quality, one he was to use to great advantage in his later years.

Carl really had something to talk about in the summer of 1853—the birth of his first child. He now had two overriding interests: mastery of the English language, and his chubby, dark-eyed daughter whom the proud parents christened Agatha.

One day this young man, whose gift of oratory "could twist the devil's tail" according to an earlier estimate, was asked by a friend to speak before a local German-American club. He had heard that the young immigrant was a well-informed person and much respected in the neighborhood for his opinions. At first, Carl was reluctant. He had fears that he might still be a "greenhorn." But when he thought of King Wilhelm's near-police state which had driven him out of his beloved Germany, he agreed. It might be a good thing to remind his listeners of conditions in their former fatherland.

Carl began on a dramatic note, a device he had learned from Kinkel. He recalled the professor's escape from prison and the "mad dash to the sea." The Germantown group was enthralled by it, just as Londoners had been. Thus encouraged, he launched into the political differences between the United States and a country ruled by an autocrat. "You disagree with something here, you vote to change it, yes! Maybe you win, maybe you lose, but nobody throws you in jail for voting against the party in power. That is not so in Germany, yes!"

The audience nodded. Carl warmed up to his challenge. He had always enjoyed public speaking; it gave him a sense of power to stand before a group and hold its attention. He lifted his head now, throwing his voice to the last row in the room. "Man is not nourished by bread alone," he concluded. "He also needs freedom, and he will find it, though he go to the ends of the earth for it!"

The answering applause filled him with confidence. For the first time since coming to America, he felt he belonged in the picture. At that precise moment, Carl Schurz stopped thinking of himself as a German. He projected himself as an *American,* a potential citizen of the United States, rather than an immigrant, bound to the past.

Not that he would forget his heritage or his mother

tongue! Far from it! But perhaps he could use his background as a bridge over which he could travel and make himself useful, as he had tonight.

After the meeting, the friend who had invited Carl to speak gave him an envelope. "Your fee for the evening, Herr Schurz. You gave us far more than we expected. I hope you'll accept this small sum with our grateful thanks."

The money was as welcome as it was unexpected. Those few dollars put an exciting new idea in his mind. He had made a living as a journalist in Europe; why not as a speaker here in America?

"Why not, indeed?" Margarethe teased on his return home. "I always knew that someday my husband would be as famous as he is handsome."

Carl was delighted when his initial success brought other offers from German-American clubs in and around Philadelphia. His fees were modest; he never earned more than ten dollars an appearance. He usually spoke in German, preferring to answer questions in English. Even then Carl Schurz sensed his future lay beyond Germantown.

However, the young orator did not delude himself. He knew that talks before local groups could not be compared to the glamorous lecture circuits so popular in the nineteenth century when men like Senator Stephen A. Douglas and Wendell Phillips, a social reformer, and Ralph Waldo Emerson, the philosopher, commanded large fees and enormous audiences.

"Your turn will come," Margarethe assured him. "How long have you been a Demosthenes . . . six months? Give yourself time, Carl. Oh, and you'd better revise your talk before the South Side *Turnverein* [a German gymnastic and social group] tomorrow night. I'm beginning to see the same familiar faces week to week."

Carl sighed. Audiences were small, fees even smaller, the travel sometimes difficult. But the experience of standing before the public was invaluable, a fact he could not appreciate until later.

He also began to attend lectures himself, traveling to New York and Baltimore to hear famous personalities discuss issues of the day. He frequently took Margarethe with him. Though not always in the best of health, she went along, aware of her husband's burning desire to understand all he could about life and events in the United States.

One paradox about the United States disturbed Carl deeply: the institution of slavery. "Intolerable!" he exploded over the paper one evening. "How can a nation which guarantees life, liberty and the pursuit of happiness harbor in its bosom slavery? When I read what this—this unspeakable Douglas says in Congress about the 'peculiar institution of slavery' and why it is needed in America—I am seeing *rote!*"

"Calm yourself, Carl," his wife replied. "The word is *red.*" She turned back to her embroidery.

"But how can a great government operate in such divided parts? North and South! Human slavery against individual freedom! This I do not understand!"

The issue which, at that moment, put the young immigrant on one side and Senator Stephen Douglas of Illinois on the other had divided an entire nation. Carl knew history well enough to realize that slavery existed in America even before the birth of the republic. Since Colonial days arguments for and against it had been waged with increasing intensity. Those in favor wanted to expand its practice to any new state that might ultimately be added to the growing nation; those against wanted to abolish slavery altogether or at least limit its spread. It was hoped that the Missouri Compromise as drawn up by Henry Clay and finally adopted by Congress in 1821 would put to rest, once and for all, its future course in the United States.

This agreement—it was, in fact, a constitutional amendment—stated that slavery could not be practiced anywhere in the vast new territories acquired through the Louisiana Purchase except *below,* or south of, the line drawn at 36 degrees, 30 minutes. Since this line was the southern boundary of Missouri, then newly formed, the state lay *above,* or north of, the compromise border. Nevertheless, after a series of bitter legislative battles, Missouri won admission to the Union as a slave state, although free Negroes could go there and live without restrictions.

All parties respected the Clay amendment for the next thirty years. No slavery was allowed above the line set by the agreement. But behind the scenes—and sometimes not too far behind—efforts were going on to modify or even repeal the law. The struggle finally came out in the open in 1854 when Stephen Douglas introduced his Kansas-Nebraska bill. In effect, this measure sought to nullify the Missouri Compromise by allowing voters in those two territories to decide for themselves whether the "peculiar institution" of slavery should be practiced within their borders. With this as precedent, a popular vote on slavery could then be taken in any state or territory, regardless of geographical position.

Carl's anger that morning was directed against the Douglas bill.

"Intolerable!" he exploded. "Slavery nursed in the cradle of freedom!" He untangled his wiry frame from a rocking chair in front of the fireplace. His moustache, started back in Switzerland as a disguise, had now grown to impressive proportions, very much in the style of the day. His wife thought he looked quite handsome in it and said so.

"Don't change the subject, Margarethe. I insist there are times when books and newspapers are not enough."

"Yes, Carl."

"There are times when a man must find things for himself out."

"That is true."

"Like seeing how lawmakers in the United States together come and decide what should be done."

Margarethe Schurz put aside her needle and embroidery hoop. "When is it you wish to leave, Carl?"

"Leave? For where?"

"Washington, of course. Isn't that where lawmakers 'together come and decide what should be done'?"

His first view of Washington, D. C., filled Carl Schurz with awe. He was, finally, at the seat of the government of his adopted land. It was from here that the President, the Congress and many federal agencies administered to the thirty-one states which then made up the Union with its nearly twenty-four million inhabitants.

The capital as it was in 1854 depressed him. The hotel in which he took a single room (Margarethe did not accompany him on this trip) was dingy beyond description, little more than a shuttered cell. The city itself reminded him of a big sprawling village, consisting of scattered groups of homes and public buildings. The streets were badly paved, if paved at all, and were frequently covered with thick dust or, after a heavy rain, puddles of mud. Public transportation was slow and undependable. "Walking is the favorite pastime here," he wrote his wife at the end of a long day of tramping. "The capital is called the city of magnificent distances, but there is nothing at the ends of those distances except a few government offices. In many of the streets geese, chickens, pigs and cows still have the right of way."

The next day, armed with letters of introduction from leaders of political clubs back in Philadelphia, Carl Schurz entered the halls of Congress. And again what he saw left him with a feeling of both elation and gloom.

The Capitol, where the Senate and House sat, was still under construction. Brick, plaster and wood gave everything a makeshift, temporary look. The Treasury Building, the White House and the Patent Office were also in various stages of construction.

Nor was he very impressed when he visited the galleries in the House of Representatives and the Senate. A man accustomed to political formality, he was shocked at the behavior and appearance of some congressmen. Many were dressed in black frock coats and satin vests, suitable enough, but more than a few sported gaudy waistcoats, in the manner of riverboat gamblers. There was also constant tobacco chewing; bright spittoons gleamed on the floors. Men talked loudly while debating was under way; some even tilted back their chairs to raise muddy boots on desks.

But Schurz had to admit that there was much genuine give-and-take. "Listening to the running debates," he wrote home that night, "I was struck by the facility of expression. The language is not always elegant or even grammatically correct; it is often blunt and rough. But it flows on without effort, and it gets to the point well enough!"

It was only later that the young immigrant understood the reasons behind this combination of apparent crudeness and political drive. The United States, after all, was then little more than sixty years old, a relatively young nation compared to the established monarchies of Europe. It was still a growing, rough-and-tumble country, a nation in a hurry. Its lawmakers came from backwoods, farms and villages as well as the larger and more sophisticated cities of the East. They had their hands full, for expansion was in the air like a great roaring wind. There just wasn't time for elegance and polished manners, the sort he had seen in Frankfurt, Paris and London.

Another aspect of the United States shocked him very much—the spoils system, the practice by which elected government officials handed out jobs to those who helped get them into office. At first, Carl Schurz did not, or perhaps would not, understand its significance.

His first experience with the spoils system came during an interview with Senator Richard Brodhead, Democrat of Pennsylvania, a stout, genial man with a shock of white hair and a low, rumbling voice. The Senator was most gracious to Schurz. He had heard that his visitor, though not yet a citizen, might well be regarded as a spokesman for the "Pennsylvania Dutch," as the German settlers in that state were sometimes called. One had to make political friends where one found them.

"Mr. Schurz," the affable Senator beamed as though Carl had been his lifelong friend. "And how are things back home, eh, with our friends and neighbors?"

"Well enough." Carl drew back, a bit puzzled by the warmth of the greeting.

"You Germans have excellent character," the lawmaker continued.

"Thank you, sir. But I came here to ask—"

"And remarkably intelligent for people who have just come to our shores. I hope, when you return to Pennsylvania, my dear Schurz, that you will remember to tell your friends of the many advantages that can be theirs under the patronage of the great Democratic party, the true peoples' party of their adopted country."

Carl thought the greeting sounded more like a political speech and almost said so. "My impression it is, Senator, that constitutional rights in the United States are granted to *all* citizens, regardless of political party, yes?"

"So they are, so they are, my boy! And you know, I wouldn't have it any other way!" The Senator narrowed his eyes. Bother this young fellow, he thought. What's his game, I wonder?

"Sir," Carl pressed forward, "would you tell me, please, where on the question of slavery you stand?"

"Slavery?" For a fleeting moment Brodhead's genial manner gave way to anger. "Well now, young man, that's a very important question, indeed, and I'm glad you asked me that. But you see, Mr. Schmidt—"

"Schurz," Carl corrected.

"You see," the other went on, refusing to acknowledge the correction, "slavery is a very complicated question. I wouldn't expect someone who's been in this country only a short while—"

"You forget, Senator, that I lived among bonded peasants in my native Germany. Men serving other men I saw, slaves serving masters!"

"Deplorable, indeed! But here in the United States"—he began edging toward the door—"we have economic conditions that are a good deal more complicated than those of Europe, so that one must look at *all* sides of the question. For which I don't have the time at the moment. However, if you want to hear about my farm program—"

Carl did not drop his level gaze, another tactic he had

Already at odds with him on the slavery issue, seeing the man and hearing him only fortified Carl's earlier opinion.

"I conceived a very strong dislike for Douglas," he wrote Margarethe. "On the floor of the Senate he spoke like a ruffian, yet with great force and cunning. I thought I recognized in him the character of a reckless, unscrupulous demagogue which, as my study of history has taught me, is so dangerous to a republic. Senator Douglas is called 'the Little Giant' with good reason. Short, stocky, and barrel-chested, he has a powerful voice and an overbearing manner. These impressions make me detest him profoundly."

Carl Schurz was to meet the Little Giant again six years later on a debating platform in Quincy, Illinois—but only as a spectator. At that time and place, the Senator had a more formidable opponent than Schurz, a man even taller, lankier, leaner.

His name was Abraham Lincoln.

4.

Grund's advice about the West haunted Carl long after he returned from Washington. The thought of open country and greater opportunity made him restless; Germantown seemed so confined compared to what lay beyond!

He was also upset and angry. The Know-Nothing party, sometimes called the American party, was then in the midst of a notorious anti-immigration campaign, especially in the East.

"I did not come to America to be persecuted again!" he growled over breakfast one day. "Look at this Boston paper!"

Margarethe glanced at the news story. A bellicose Know-Nothing leader, whose parents had come from Europe only two generations before, was demanding that aliens now living in the United States wait twenty-one years for citizenship instead of the normal five-year period. He also urged that employment be given only to natural-born citizens. In passing, he dropped several strong anti-Catholic insults, all part and parcel of the Know-Nothing platform.

"It is only a phase," Margarethe answered. "It will pass."

"It will get worse! *Know-Nothings!* A proper name!"

The name described the *behavior* of party members rather than their lack of knowledge. As a secret society, they conducted their meetings behind closed doors. Members were forbidden to talk to outsiders about the group's mystic rites and rituals. When pressed for details, their only response was an automatic "I know nothing about them," thus giving the organization its popular name.

"If they had their way," Carl fumed, "we would all be packing for Europe! Margarethe—" he suddenly changed his voice, "they tell me that in the West there are no such feelings about immigrants, that one can be a citizen without too much difficulty, even one who has trouble yet with the English language!"

Margarethe sighed. That tone and that look, she knew them both. She also knew it would be only a matter of weeks before he was on the move again.

A month later, she was helping him pack. Carl had, in the meantime, hired himself out as an agent for a gas company. Now he was about to make a tour of the West—in those days, anything on the other side of Pennsylvania was "the West" —to interest towns and cities in the installation of gas street-lighting systems. His real target, however, was a home beyond the Alleghenies.

That first day on the train he never took his eyes off the countryside. At night he passed through Pittsburgh, whose streets glowed from the light of bonfires, a precaution against cholera. In the morning, the train sped through the dense forests of Ohio; in the evening it rolled through miles of verdant farmlands. Then, as the train approached Cincinnati, the "Queen City of the West," Carl felt a pang of homesickness. The Ohio River might easily have been the Rhine!

He shook himself back to reality with the reminder that his future lay here, in the America of the rural wilderness, not back in the Rhine Valley—or even Philadelphia. Of that he felt certain.

The train sped on to Indianapolis, to St. Louis, Chicago and Milwaukee. At each stop Carl dutifully saw city officials and presented his message in behalf of the gas company. Then at night he wrote long letters to Margarethe.

"The plains of Indiana depress me," he confided. "I could never live on such unbroken, unending meadows." St. Louis he found more congenial, "but they say it is dreadfully hot in summer and there is much malaria here." Chicago he described as "already too big and bustling, and too full of rats and bedbugs." Milwaukee, he wrote, was "too full of Germans. I have not heard two words of English since my arrival yesterday."

One community finally captured his eye and heart—Watertown, Wisconsin, some forty-five miles west of Milwaukee. "This small city is located on a gentle river from which Watertown gets its name," he explained in an enthusiastic letter, "a picturesque, lively town of some 8,500 people. Margarethe, I have at last found our future home!"

Within a year the Schurzes had moved to Watertown where Carl bought a large, rambling farmhouse on ninety acres of land overlooking the river. The purchase was made possible by a big mortgage and Margarethe's dowry, a generous gift from her father at the time of her marriage three years before. The move west was almost a small caravan, including as it did the young couple, their infant daughter, Carl's parents and his two sisters.

The entire family now buckled down to work. Carl's father was put in charge of the farm and small dairy; his mother and sisters kept chickens and worked the large vegetable garden. Carl himself began to study law. In those days, law schools were rare. Candidates for the bar, especially in rural areas, prepared themselves by reading, attending court and clerking for local attorneys.

Carl began to study Blackstone, the great authority on English law; he read Thomas Jefferson, Benjamin Franklin,

John Adams and Thomas Paine. A volume of the *Federalist Papers* was his constant companion. Through these books he learned more about American history, about the rights of man and the moral basis of law as practiced in Western civilization.

Margarethe, too, was busy with her large house and small child. Finding it easier to keep the two-year-old Agatha occupied if other children were present, she called in youngsters from neighboring houses. Soon she was running a nursery, much like the schools for very little children that she had seen in Germany. She gave her project the German name *Kindergarten,* literally "a garden for little ones." So, while her husband studied law, Margarethe Schurz established America's first kindergarten in her Watertown home. The modest fee she charged helped support her family during those first years in Wisconsin.

Carl, meanwhile, traveled frequently to Madison, the state capital, about a day's journey by horseback. Here he sat in on sessions of the various courts, the more the better. He visited the state university there; and he talked—with lawyers, judges, editors, professors, anyone who could feed his insatiable hunger for knowledge. He also became a notary and land agent, and thus made himself better known in the community, particularly among the many German-Americans in the area.

Carl was also gregarious. He thrived on people and politics. After studying all day, he made it a habit to amble down to the center of Watertown and exchange views with friends and neighbors. These informal gatherings were held outdoors in summer, with the men sprawled out on cracker boxes, logs or stumps. In winter, they adjourned to the post office or general store where the give and take went on around sizzling potbellied stoves.

The young law student thoroughly enjoyed these sessions. Each man was on his own, free to say what he pleased. But he had better come prepared to back up his statements. Though untutored for the most part, these men had a native intelligence that quickly nailed down exaggerations and false premises. As one of the more active members of the village forum, Carl had to be constantly on his toes. Also, his law studies added to his stature; his opinions and comments were closely followed by the townspeople.

One of the burning issues of the day was slavery, as it had been from the time Carl Schurz first landed in America. The farmers and merchants of Watertown were as keen on the topic as the abolitionists back East. Discussions that summer centered around the Kansas-Nebraska Act, which was passed in May, 1854, and which, in effect, had done away with the Missouri Compromise. Carl was strongly against the bill; so were most of his fellow townspeople. But he, better than most, was able to say exactly why.

"It's the old cause of human freedom," he explained. "Where one man leads, another follows, and pretty soon you have political organizations, some for an issue, some against. And it's up to you and me to take a stand." By now Carl could speak English fluently, with a slight accent. "That's why the Republican party was formed, to give folks a chance to vote against this cruel business of slavery, if they have a mind to. That's why I'm supporting it, though I won't be able to vote until next year. When I get my citizenship papers, you bet I will!"

The men in the circle nodded gravely. A few had already joined the new political party organized two years before in nearby Ripon. From there the Republican movement had spread, bringing together antislavery Democrats, Free-Soil party members and what was left of the northern Whigs. By the summer of 1856, the Republicans had a national organization, a platform, and a presidential candidate—General John C. Frémont, the "Pathfinder," called that because of his explorations in the Far West.

Carl pounded his palm earnestly. "It's going to be Frémont against Buchanan, freedom against slavery, Republicans against Democrats next November! What I wouldn't give to be able to vote!"

Among those listening to him that pleasant summer evening was a stranger who had just arrived in Watertown. His name was L. P. Harvey, a state senator and chairman of the Republican party in Wisconsin, who had come to town to line up support for Frémont. Imagine his surprise when he found someone doing the job for him, and doing it where it counted most—at the grass roots level!

Senator Harvey, a shrewd politician, liked what he heard. After the meeting broke up, he introduced himself to the tall young man who had been the center of attraction. "Will you join me in a pipe, friend? I find your arguments very persuasive."

Carl smiled, pleased at the compliment. "It's late, Senator. My wife thinks I do too much talking as it is."

"Too late to discuss the future of our party?"

Carl's eyes crinkled in pleasure. "Never too late for politics!"

The two men sat in the cozy taproom of the Watertown Hotel long past midnight. Finally Senator Harvey put the question to him. "We need people like you, Mr. Schurz, to speak to groups throughout Wisconsin. Funny thing about rural folk. They'll listen to one of their own a lot sooner than they will to some politician from the big city. Like tonight on the village green. You had them eating out of your hand. So what do you say, friend? We'll pay all your expenses plus five dollars a day."

Before answering, Carl recalled the advice given him two years ago by Francis Grund: "The West is growing . . . it will give you a chance to grow with it." He tamped down his pipe, then blew out a cloud of smoke.

"What do you want me to do, Senator, and when can I start?"

The hard-working Schurz proved to be a boon for Wisconsin Republicans. He was constantly on the move. One day he addressed factory workers in Milwaukee. The next day he spoke to dairymen in Janesville, after which he packed his bag for a trip up north where he spoke to farmers, loggers and villagers. He spoke in both English and German, depending on his audiences. It was a rough-and-tumble campaign. There were times when he was challenged by hecklers who threw not only insults at him but an occasional vegetable or two. But he was quick on his feet, and his earnest appeals turned many a German-American's vote in Frémont's favor. Above all, he gained in both experience and confidence.

No one really expected the Republicans to win the 1856 election, but few expected them to do as well as they did. A new party with new leadership, they made an excellent showing, winning 114 electoral votes to 174 for Buchanan.

Carl should have been pleased since Wisconsin went for Frémont, a fact which did not escape Senator Harvey. "We did well," he consoled the young campaigner.

"We lost," Schurz answered. "What does it take to convince people, anyway? How could they possibly choose slavery over liberty?"

"It takes organization, Carl. And hard work, the kind you did so well for us."

"Not an issue, Senator? Not a cause?"

"Not always. In politics, a well-oiled party machine counts for more than a trunkful of ideals. You'll understand that in time. That is, if you'll stick to the game."

"It must not be a game." Carl shook his head, seeing more in the defeat of Frémont than a party setback. It was a blow against reason, against any civilized approach to the question of slavery.

"I cannot understand," he wrote Kinkel a few days later, "how politicians fail to see right from wrong. They only see victory or defeat. Let them win at the polls and their cause becomes right. So it is with Buchanan's victory, *ergo* slavery becomes right. This is specious reasoning, as you have taught me. And, as cause follows effect, as you also have taught me, then I can say, unhappily, that the time for compromise has passed and the last chance for a peaceful solution of the slavery issue has come and gone."

Less than five years later, his prediction was to become a terrible reality.

Carl's outlook brightened considerably that winter with the birth of another daughter; she was named Marianne, after his mother. He also passed his bar examinations. However, he had found another interest by now—journalism.

His new career was the direct result of the recent elections. Carl had taken the trouble to write out his speeches so that local papers were supplied with copies even before he spoke. "I not only want to be quoted," he explained, "but I want to be quoted right." Not even opposition papers could distort his remarks once he had put them on the record.

His speeches were models of logical construction, written

in language that was clear and to the point. "You have a gift for the written word," Harvey had encouraged him during the campaign. "Perhaps the party can do something with it after the elections."

The party did. Hoping to hold on to the large German-American vote in southern Wisconsin, the Republicans started a German-language newspaper, the Watertown *Deutsche Volks-Zeitung,* literally translated to mean the "German Peoples' News."

The logical choice for editor was Carl Schurz.

"I will accept on one condition, Senator Harvey," Carl agreed. "The paper must be independent. If my views coincide with those of the party—and I think they will most of the time—well and good. If they do not, I must have freedom to dissent."

The veteran politician let out a sigh. Better to have this editorial tiger on a leash than lose him to some other cause. "Mr. Schurz," he stuck out his hand, "you have a deal!"

In the first issue, editor Schurz proudly announced that his publication would be "independent but not neutral," and promptly came out with an antislavery policy that went beyond anything put forward by Wisconsin Republicans. Senator Harvey had no objections. He was more concerned with local issues than with national affairs. As long as Schurz kept the state machine supplied with readers, and therefore potential voters, he was doing his job.

Carl had a busy and happy time with his newspaper. As a local publication, the *Volks-Zeitung* carried many items concerned only with affairs in southern Wisconsin. But the editor made sure that the question of slavery never languished; he also commented on news from Washington and Europe. When a visiting lecturer came through, he was interviewed extensively. Soon his little paper began to draw statewide attention among German-speaking audiences. "We could do worse than run Schurz for office," Senator Harvey confided to the party leadership. "The only thing is, how well can we control him?"

He decided to find out.

When the state elections of 1857 approached, he paid another visit to Watertown. There he found the lanky editor looking over page proofs of his latest issue. "Carl," the Senator began, "how would you like to *make* news instead of just writing it?"

Schurz pushed back his green eyeshade. "What do you mean, Senator?"

"I mean how would you like to run for state office? The party's prepared to back you up, all the way!"

He thought it over for a moment. "What's open, Senator?"

Harvey showed him the slate of offices that would be on the ticket that fall. Carl ran his eyes over the list, rubbed his chin for a moment, then decided he would gamble for the number two post.

"I'd like to run for . . . lieutenant-governor!" If Harvey objected, he could always work his way down.

The Senator didn't bat an eyelash. He liked confidence in young politicians. "Sure thing. I'll recommend you to the nominating committee."

Next week, Carl himself wrote the front page story for his paper. "Carl Schurz, editor of the *Deutsche Volks-Zeitung,* announced his candidacy today for the office of lieutenant-governor of Wisconsin on the Republican ticket. . . ." He looked up, a slow smile spreading over his sharp features.

Not bad, he thought, for a former greenhorn who had just become a United States citizen and had yet to reach his thirtieth birthday!

Carl's acceptance speech later that month before convention delegates made them sit up and take notice. "I accept the nomination in the cause of freedom," he proclaimed, "freedom apart from party, apart from local issues, apart from partisan politics." When he concluded, the crowd gave him an ovation. Carl Schurz had come to the convention as only a name; he was leaving it very much a political reality.

The candidate's zeal was not entirely to Harvey's liking. "Give them more about what they want to hear, Carl!" the Senator advised. "Talk to them about post offices and farm programs and less about the law of the land. Don't preach to them! Reach them! Promise them something they're looking for, something they can grab on to and maybe put in their pockets! That's the way to get votes!"

Carl tried to oblige, even though Harvey's advice sounded much like the "spoils system" philosophy he detested. Once when he spoke in La Crosse on the necessity of expanding commerce along the upper Mississippi River—the western border of Wisconsin—a heckler interrupted him. He reminded Carl that free northern trade could never compete with slave trade, and that it would be much more profitable to adopt the labor practices of the South. "That's the way to build up the economy, mister!"

The man was baiting him, and Carl knew it. Keeping control of his temper, he set aside his prepared remarks and carefully pointed out that it was as wrong morally to spend a dollar earned at the expense of human slavery as it was to pass a counterfeit bill—perhaps even more so.

Senator Harvey winced. "A man like that," he whispered to an aide, "sure makes a fellow agree if he's already leaning that way. But if he isn't—!"

His worst fears were realized on election day. Wisconsin Republicans put all their candidates in office except one man

—Carl Schurz. He lost his race by the narrow margin of forty-eight votes. Party leaders guessed at the reason—he simply wouldn't play politics, wouldn't make promises and wouldn't stop talking about slavery.

"More's the pity," they mourned. "To have a vote-getter like that go down, just because he won't compromise. Don't make sense." The regret was genuine. Even a rival newspaper, the Watertown *Democrat,* conceded that he had been the "ablest and most eloquent" speaker in the campaign and that the best man, indeed, had not won.

Most regretful of all was Senator Harvey. He had taken a real fancy to that young man, even thought of him as his successor in the state senate one day. "All you had to do was go easy on slavery. But no. You had to go all out. It nailed down your defeat, I'm sure it did."

Carl nodded. "So am I, Senator. But I couldn't do it any other way. Winning at any price is not my idea of victory."

Later that night, he consoled himself with a comment he was to remember long after his Wisconsin defeat was forgotten. "Nothing that is wrong in principle," Schurz wrote in his journal, "can ever be right in practice."

5. The defeated candidate returned to Watertown to find himself something of a celebrity. Although campaign oratory had failed to put him in office, it had, nevertheless, made him a prime attraction for the lecture circuit, or the lyceum, as it was called in those days. Invitations to speak for pay began to pour in.

Schurz accepted gladly, since his small newspaper barely made expenses. Also, lecturing gave him the opportunity to do what he most enjoyed—write, travel and meet people. His fee for these "one-night stands" was fifty dollars, often less.

Those were the golden days of the lyceum. People traveled for miles to pay for the privilege of listening to experts talk on politics, history, music or art. The speaking platform was often their only contact with the outside world.

Carl built his lectures around the subject of "True Americanism," which he defined as "the responsible attitude of citizens and government to the laws of the land." He was an imposing figure behind the lectern, thanks to his bushy beard and professorial manner which made him look far older than his thirty years. His delivery, however, was warm and simple. He never ranted or used cheap theatrics, but made his points clearly and logically. And he never talked down to his audience. Another factor in his favor was his ability to speak equally well in German or English.

Always a perfectionist, he wrote down every word of his

speeches, memorizing each important point so that he could look directly at his listeners and thus fill them with the same confidence he had instilled in himself. Behind his skilled oratory was the excellence of a masterful pen.

Schurz's reputation as a speaker soon spread to neighboring states. In September, 1858, he was asked to address a mass meeting in Mechanics Hall in Chicago, sponsored by the supporters of Abraham Lincoln. At that time Lincoln, a country lawyer little known outside his native Illinois, was running for United States senator against the more prominent Stephen A. Douglas.

The background for the occasion was perfect for a man of Carl's convictions. Leveling his sights on the Little Giant, as Douglas was sometimes called, Schurz delivered a devastating attack on the author of the proslavery Kansas-Nebraska bill. "The contest between Lincoln and Douglas is, in every sense of the word," he proclaimed, "the prelude to the irrepressible conflict."

The Chicago talk created a sensation. Its effects were felt as far as the influential East. "Carl Schurz," Horace Greeley wrote in his New York *Tribune,* "speaks with an eloquence, force and intelligence which prove him an invaluable acquisition to his adopted country." Privately, Greeley confided to his political associates, men high in liberal Republican ranks, that the midwestern editor was a man well worth watching.

A million copies of Schurz's Chicago talk, appropriately entitled "The Irrepressible Conflict," were printed and distributed. It made him into a national, if somewhat youthful, political figure almost overnight. In an indirect way, it also brought him into contact with Abraham Lincoln, whose gaunt figure was just beginning to cast its fateful shadow across the land.

The meeting between them took place on October 13,

1858, on a train bound for Quincy, Illinois. Carl was on his way there to lecture and was dozing fitfully, trying to catch up on lost sleep, when the train door opened and shouts of "Hey, Abe! Hullo, Abe!" awakened him. He looked up, somewhat dazed. There, standing in the aisle, was a tall, lean man with hollow cheeks and eyes sunk deep in a swarthy face. On top of a large head obviously in need of a haircut perched a dusty stovepipe hat. In one hand the gangling figure carried a battered satchel; a gray woolen shawl hung from the other arm. But it was the man's moody countenance, with its lined face, large nose, huge ears and sad, sad eyes, that held Carl's attention. Was *this* the Abraham Lincoln revered by Republicans throughout Illinois?

He must be, Carl decided, for shouts of "Ole Abe!" continued until that lanky individual, with the slightest gesture, brought the demonstration to a close. "I understand," he began in a quiet, high-pitched voice so unlike his rugged appearance, "that Carl Schurz is somewhere in this car. Would one of you gentlemen be good enough to introduce me to him?"

A startled Schurz jumped to his feet, for once at a loss for words.

Introductions were quickly made by political friends. "Mighty glad to catch up with you, Mr. Schurz," Lincoln began after a warm handshake. "Here, let's set a while and get to know one t'other." Offering Carl the window seat, he stretched his long legs out in the aisle. "You a country man, sir?"

"I own ninety acres in Wisconsin," his puzzled guest answered. "Farm most of it, too."

"Good. Then you know what rain can do for crops."

"Y—yes." What was the man driving at?

"When it falls at the right time, the growing season,"

Lincoln elaborated, "it brings life and new energy. But at the wrong time, say the haying season, rain means disaster, right?" A large hand fell on Carl's knee as if to confirm the statement. "That's the way I calculated your Chicago talk, Mr. Schurz. Your 'Irrepressible Conflict' speech came just at the right time for me, right in the middle of Old Abe's growing season. And for that, I'm much obliged."

"Old Abe," though only ten years Carl's senior, looked far older. Rough, grotesque in appearance, given to rustic homilies, but direct and friendly—that was the impression Carl Schurz had of Lincoln that day and he was never to change it.

The two met again twenty months later in Springfield, Illinois, this time on a much more formal occasion. Both men, in the interim, had come a long way in their respective careers.

Schurz's small German-language journal had extended his reputation far beyond Watertown; other papers frequently translated his editorials and published them as outstanding examples of Republican thinking. He had also developed into a fine orator, as well known in the East as the Midwest. His most recent speaking triumph had taken him to Boston where he delivered a powerful indictment of the Know-Nothings when that movement showed signs of revival. Editor William Lloyd Garrison called that speech "one of the most eloquent that has ever been made in Faneuil Hall in fifty years."

Schurz went to Chicago for the 1860 Republican National Convention as chairman of the Wisconsin delegation. He also served on the party's Committee on Resolutions, two responsible leadership posts.

As for Lincoln, he had sunk back into anonymity after his defeat by Douglas two years before. But his followers would not desert him and insisted on entering his name as a presidential candidate in the convention which, that year, was held in a hideously massive wooden structure called The Wigwam.

The balloting began with William Seward well out in front. As the choice of the affluent East, he had come to Chicago with the nomination all but tucked away in his vest pocket. But he couldn't pull away from Lincoln, who drew strong support from midwestern states. When the latter picked up important strength on the second ballot, the convention was faced with a virtual deadlock.

Schurz had come to The Wigwam fully prepared to support Seward. When he saw that Thurlow Weed, an unscrupulous New York journalist and politician, was pulling convention strings for Seward, he began to have second thoughts.

The third ballot opened on an ominous note—for Seward. The Ohio delegation, which had previously backed favorite son Salmon Chase, shifted four votes to Lincoln. Only a slight advantage for the dark horse from Springfield, but the wheels of his bandwagon were beginning to roll. Now state after state began to climb aboard; soon the stampede was on.

This was just the sort of opportunity Schurz was waiting for. Jumping to his feet at the height of the wild excitement, he seconded the motion that Lincoln be made the unanimous choice of the convention, a motion that was promptly carried out by the jubilant delegates. And it was Schurz again who was named to the select group of party leaders who journeyed to Springfield to notify the victor of his nomination. On that second meeting, by no means the last between the two, Carl was struck at how much older and more melancholy the man appeared. "The nickname Old Abe really suits him now," he wrote his wife from Springfield. "It is as if the weight of the entire nation is carried on his lean shoulders. As for myself, I have reason to feel much gratified at his nomination."

Now began a frantic round of political activity for Schurz. Appointed a member of the Republican National Executive Committee, his most important job was to swing the votes of foreign-born citizens, chiefly Germans, Scandinavians and Dutch, to the Republican candidate. "I shall do the work of a hundred men for your election," he wrote Lincoln, "and go anywhere in your behalf." To which the latter replied that he was most grateful and added: "To the extent of our limited acquaintance, no man stands nearer to my heart than yourself."

All through that hot summer and early fall, Carl Schurz carried the party message to more than two million naturalized citizens who, in many states, held the balance of power at the polls. To the national committee, he said: "If a considerable number of foreign-born voters who usually vote Democratic can be converted to our cause, Lincoln stands better than an even chance of winning." Toward this end he delivered dozens of speeches in the small cities of the Midwest, then traveled to Boston, New York and Philadelphia for more campaigning.

To his audiences he pleaded: "The purely moral motive in any election has never been so strong. We must make this the revolt of the popular conscience against the great wrong of slavery. Our cause, now as always, must be based on liberty, right and justice!"

These campaign tours added to Carl's political and intellectual maturity. He met with such prominent figures as Salmon P. Chase, the financier and later Chief Justice of the Supreme Court, and with Senator Charles Sumner, of Massachusetts, the dedicated abolitionist, with whom he was to have a close friendship for many years. In New England, he talked intimately with Dr. Oliver Wendell Holmes, the father of the future jurist, with naturalist Louis Agassiz and with such noted writers as Henry Wadsworth Longfellow, Ralph Waldo Emerson and John Greenleaf Whittier. With all of them he shared one thing in common—the concern for human freedom: "Not with an effort of saying anything remarkable," as he later wrote in his autobiography, but sharing with them "the natural, unpretending and therefore the most charming simplicity of truly great minds."

In the meantime, the campaign continued without letup. Two months before election, Schurz and Lincoln held a long strategy talk in Springfield, at which time the presidential candidate suggested that Carl swing through the Midwest once again. "But not to the cities this time," Lincoln pointed out dolefully. "I want you to campaign in the backwoods, the sticks, where no railroad has ever been. Feel up to making the rural run, Carl?"

When Schurz nodded that he did—how he wished he were home now with his wife and children!—Lincoln added: "Men like you who have real merit are always too proud to ask for anything. You may depend on this—when the time comes I shall know how to tell deserving men from drones."

Carl all but forgot this remark as the campaign whirled on. He traveled by stagecoach and horseback over country roads; he slept in small inns and farmhouses. Sometimes he even went out to the fields and spoke to groups of farmers during their midday meals. Then, as election day neared, he was sent back to the large cities for more rallies. He found himself in "the thick of the fight," as he wrote Margarethe. "The blows I have delivered in Lincoln's behalf were glorious . . . it seems as if victory could not fail us!"

Victory did not. Lincoln was elected, perhaps due as much

to the fact that the Democrats were split (they had three presidential candidates in 1860, including Stephen A. Douglas) as to the great moral issue of slavery which Carl Schurz articulated so effectively. In the opinion of several prominent historians, Schurz's contribution in the campaign was significant, even decisive.

That winter Carl devoted his time to his family and his newspaper, both neglected for many months. Then in March, 1861, a letter bearing the return address of "A. Lincoln, President of the United States" was delivered to his Watertown address just as he was sitting down to breakfast.

Carl opened it and read the single, hand-written page.

"Something important?" Margarethe asked. "Anything that concerns us and the children?"

Carl set his cup down with a slow smile. "I should think so, yes. It's a note from Old Abe. He wants to know how I'd feel about accepting an appointment as the Ambassador to Spain."

Carl and Margarethe Schurz, together with their two children, sailed from New York in June, 1861, bound for Europe. But the excitement of the voyage was somewhat tempered for the young ambassador by two recent decisions. He had reluctantly agreed that his wife should continue on to Germany where she and the two girls would stay with friends, while he remained in Madrid. Margarethe suffered greatly in excessive heat, and she was afraid the hot Spanish summers might be too much for her. Moreover, the situation at home had changed greatly.

As the steamer glided out of the bay, Carl, now a mature thirty-two, reflected on his second decision. The ambassadorship to Spain had seemed a splendid opportunity only a few short months ago. But that assignment had suddenly lost its appeal with the first shot fired on Fort Sumter on April 12,

1861, signaling the start of the Civil War between the North and the South. Carl had pleaded at once for military duty, but Lincoln persuaded him that the Madrid post was important and that someone dependable had to be kept abroad "to keep an eye on European reaction to our troubles at home," as he put it. Carl had finally dropped his objections and agreed to serve overseas.

He now looked back from the stern of the ship. Nine short years before he had come to America as a "greenhorn," a political refugee from the Old World. Now he was returning to Europe as an official Ambassador of the United States government with full diplomatic rank and status. He glanced down once more at the leather dispatch case given him as a gift from his friends in Watertown. On it, in bold golden letters, he read, for perhaps the hundredth time:

"Carl Schurz, Minister Plenipotentiary and Envoy Extraordinary to Spain."

6. Once in Madrid, the young American official threw himself eagerly into his diplomatic duties. However, the news from home was distracting. The European press described the First Battle of Bull Run, which took place on July 21, 1861, as "not only a catastrophe, but even a disgrace to Northern arms." The fact that some Northern soldiers had turned tail and run off was reported in the Spanish press, with appropriate jokes about the sprinting ability of Yankee troops.

Carl winced at the cruel jibes. If only he could be home, leading troops in battle! It seemed to him now that his country needed his sword much more than his diplomatic pen. Accordingly, he studied books on military strategy instead of wining and dining at night with his ambassadorial colleagues. With every report to Washington he sent along an urgent request: *I beg to be relieved of my present assignment in favor of a military post in the field!*

His repeated entreaties were finally answered. Carl Schurz was ordered home for consultation. Remaining in Madrid only long enough for Margarethe and the two children to join him from Germany, the impatient diplomat booked passage on the first vessel bound for America. An hour after landing in New York on February 2, 1862, he was on his way to the nation's capital.

"The true place for a young and able-bodied man," he impressed on President Lincoln, "is in the field and not in an easy chair."

Lincoln nodded, his appearance now made even more melancholy by a dark beard. "Your request, Mr. Ambassador," he reminded Carl, "means giving up a large salary and a distinguished post in exchange for hard work, discomfort and danger." When Schurz could not be talked out of his resolve, a small smile began to break the President's solemnity. "I expected this, Carl, and I have already sent your name to the Senate with the next batch of brigadier generals for confirmation. In the meantime, there are a couple of things that need looking after. . . ."

Carl responded with an enthusiasm not at all becoming a former diplomat. First he deposited his wife and children in a rented home near Bethlehem, Pennsylvania, where Margarethe had a distant cousin. Carl reasoned she would be less lonely there than in Watertown, where his parents still maintained his house. Furthermore, Bethlehem was only a few hours by rail from Washington, D.C., and Virginia, where the bulk of the Northern forces were quartered. It would be a simple matter for him to visit his family whenever he was granted leave, even for a few days. Wisconsin, at that time, seemed very far off, both as to distance and as the focus of interest.

Carl's first assignment was to organize battalions of German-American troops, a job for which he was uniquely qualified. He also screened a number of former German officers who had flocked to America at the outbreak of the Civil War, some of whom had fought at his side in the 1848 revolution. The Northern officer ranks soon boasted the names of men Schurz recommended for duty: General Franz Sigel, General Adolf Steinwher, Colonel Alexander von Schimmelfennig, Colonel Leopold von Gilsa and others who served on the Union forces with distinction.

Another of Lincoln's requests sent Schurz back to the speaking platform. He went to New York to address a large antislavery meeting at Cooper Union, then one of the best-known lecture halls in the East. His speech before a jammed auditorium, called "Reconciliation by Emancipation," was one of his great oratorical efforts. Its most important point was that the Union could not be restored, even after the Southern rebellion was put down, unless slavery was abolished everywhere. But Schurz was no extremist like some of the other abolitionists, notably Charles Sumner. He suggested as a start that slavery be abolished in the District of Columbia as an example to the entire nation. He also proposed that only slaves of avowed rebels be set free at the onset, and that fair compensation be offered to other slave masters if they would agree to emancipation by degrees.

No sooner had Schurz finished his moderate proposals, than Horace Greeley stepped onto the platform, waving a yellow piece of paper. "I have just received a wire from President Lincoln," he told a suddenly hushed audience, "announcing that he will send to Congress a special message offering gradual emancipation and with complete compensation to slave owners. It seems, ladies and gentlemen, that our principal speaker and the President of the United States are of one mind!"

The drama hit the audience with telling effect. Carl Schurz had spoken, Abraham Lincoln had acted! Both men were wildly cheered.

Ironically, nothing came of the proposal, even though Congress promptly adopted the resolution. To Carl's sorrow—and undoubtedly Lincoln's—not a single slave-owning state responded to the President's offer. The struggle between the North and the South had become too involved to be undone by the pen.

The sword was now the only weapon.

Brigadier General Carl Schurz took the field at Harrisonburg, Virginia, on June 10, 1862, reporting to Major General John C. Frémont, the same man for whom he had stumped in the presidential elections of 1856. His divisional command was made up of two regiments from New York, two from Pennsylvania, one from Ohio, one from West Virginia and two artillery batteries and a cavalry company. Most of his men and officers were of German descent. For this reason they were called, sometimes disparagingly, "Schurz's Dutchmen."

Carl stepped into uniform at a particularly bad time for the North. General McClellan, as head of the Union forces, was bogged down in the Virginia swamps. His movements were indecisive, the morale of his troops low. Too, there was jealousy on the staff level. "Political" generals like Schurz were looked down upon by regular army officers who had graduated from the war college at West Point. As a result, the course of military affairs suffered.

However, General Schurz refused to become discouraged. He moved among the ranks, drilled his men firmly and soon won their admiration as a fair and untiring commander. He brought a semblance of order to his troops in a war where the flow of supplies and equipment were often in the hands of profiteers and seldom delivered on time or in the quantities specified. With his insistence on discipline, his "Dutchmen" soon proved to be one of the best-trained divisions in the field.

Though now behind the sword, Carl Schurz did not neglect his pen. Observant and intelligent as always, he left behind a detailed account of military action as he experienced it on the field.

Of a forced march in the heat of August, he wrote: "There was not a cloud in the sky, and no breath of air stirring. The dust raised by the marching column enveloped the men like a dense, dark, immovable fog bank. As the heat grew fiercer, the troops, burdened with their knapsacks and blankets, their guns and cartridge belts, with faces streaming with sweat, their mouths and nostrils filled with earthy slime . . . their eyes wide open with a sort of insane stare, dragged themselves along. . . ."

When Stonewall Jackson's rear guard suddenly turned on his advancing division during a skirmish at Freedom's Ford, Schurz penned this frank account: "My Eighth Virginia broke and ran. My first service on the battlefield thus consisted in stopping and rallying broken troops, which I and my officers did with drawn swords and lively language."

Later, he confessed: "I remember to have been at one time continually in the saddle for more than thirty hours . . . it was then that I learned to sleep on horseback."

Of the irony of battle, he wrote: "On the 11th [of August] we had a day's truce between the two armies [Stonewall Jackson's of the South, General Banks' of the North] for the purpose of caring for the wounded and burying the dead. Confederate and Union officers met on the battlefield of Cedar Mountain and exchanged polite compliments."

The compassionate Schurz recalled the aftermath of still another battle: "The stretchers coming in dreadful procession from the bloody field, their bloodstained burdens to be unloaded at the places where the surgeons stand with their medicine chests and bandages, and their knives and uprolled sleeves and blood-smeared aprons, and by their ghastly heaps of cut-off legs and arms—and oh, the shrieks and wailings of the wounded men as they are handled by the attendants, and the beseeching eyes of the dying boy who says with his broken voice: 'Oh, General, can you not do something for me?' I can do nothing but stroke his hands and utter some words of hope—which I do not believe myself. . . ."

"War," General William Tecumseh Sherman was supposed to have said, "is hell!" Actually what he said was: "War is cruelty, and you cannot refine it."

Carl Schurz could not have agreed more. Whatever romantic notions of the sword he might have retained from his early days were now blasted in the face of war's reality. And reality, as he saw it, was made up of equal parts of bravery and inefficiency, especially inefficiency in high places.

Once, exasperated by what seemed to him a string of futile military maneuvers, Carl Schurz wrote to President Lincoln complaining that the war might go better for the North if certain key officers put their "hearts into the common effort."

Lincoln's reply was prompt, brusque, and to the point. Hard-pressed by the thousand details of administering a nation at war—the Emancipation Proclamation had already been issued—he reminded Schurz that he, Lincoln, was perfectly satisfied with his general staff and that if Schurz really wanted to move the war along, he had best stick to his job, which was to look after his own troops.

Looking back on this incident, history seems to justify Schurz's impatience, though not his diplomacy. The fact is that Lincoln repeatedly changed command of the Army of the Potomac, as one general after another led Northern troops into indecisive, and sometimes even disastrous, military campaigns. As a matter of record, it wasn't until General Grant was brought in from the West—long after Schurz wrote his letter—that the Northern army began to move with purpose. Furthermore, in a subsequent meeting, the President himself suggested that his reproof was intended to keep the impatient Schurz from upsetting the line of command, not to put him in his place. Indeed, they parted "the best of friends," according to Carl's diary.

Schurz always spoke of Lincoln in the highest terms; he was one of the Chief Executive's few contemporaries who recognized greatness in the shaggy, melancholy occupant of the White House. "The President is a man of profound feeling," Carl wrote to an old university friend, "with just and firm principles, and incorruptible integrity. He is the people personified; that is the secret of his popularity. In fifty years, perhaps much sooner, Lincoln's name will stand written upon the honor roll of the American Republic, next to that of Washington, and there it will remain for all time."

At that time, in the midst of a great war and during the height of Lincoln's harassment by generals and politicians alike, that letter seemed like an absurd prophecy.

Except for a brief period in the fall of 1864, when he took the campaign trail for Lincoln's re-election, Carl Schurz remained in uniform until the very end of the Civil War. He was General Slocum's chief of staff and was advancing with him on Raleigh, North Carolina, when General Robert E. Lee of the Confederate Army surrendered with full military honors to General Ulysses S. Grant at Appomattox on April 9, 1865.

No one could have foreseen the terrible tragedy that followed so soon after the surrender of the South. Lincoln was then at the height of his popularity, having defeated General George McClellan, the former Union commander, for the Presidency the year before. McClellan came up with the idea of the absentee ballot for members of the armed forces. Sensing that the North was tired of war, he had pressed for an absentee vote for soldiers during the 1864 campaign, convinced that his former comrades-in-arms would support him, since his election promise was a quick and negotiated end to the fighting.

Some 150,000 absentee ballots were sent in from the field. Much to McClellan's dismay, more than three-quarters of the soldier vote went to Lincoln. The Union Army, as well as the nation, it seemed, wanted the conflict pressed to the end.

So when, on April 14, 1865, less than a week after the surrender at Appomattox, Lincoln was shot down by an assassin in Ford's Theater, the nation was thrown into shock. "The murderer who did this deed," Schurz wrote to his wife when the President died the following day, "has killed the best friend of the South . . . our triumph is no longer jubilant."

Carl Schurz left the military with "a profound abhorrence of war as such," the last entry he made in his war diary. Unlike other political figures of his day, he seldom used the title "General." Given the choice between the pen and the sword, he had already decided which he would use in his fight for freedom.

7. Like many other ex-soldiers returning from the war, Carl Schurz found himself in an economic bind. There was now one more mouth to feed; his wife had given birth to another daughter, Emma Savannah, on December 30, 1865. Also, a series of poor land investments, made just before the war, had depleted his bank account. To make matters worse, the holder of the mortgage on the family home in Watertown sued for foreclosure. It was not likely that Carl could return to a well-paying post in public life. Lincoln was dead, and with him all hopes of another appointment comparable to his position as Ambassador to Spain.

A short-term offer filled the gap, however. Andrew Johnson, who had succeeded to the Presidency, asked Schurz to tour the South and report on what steps might be taken in the reconstruction of that area. The President's choice of a man associated with the Radical Republicans—his avowed political enemies—seems puzzling at first. But perhaps "Andy" Johnson remembered that Schurz and Lincoln once enjoyed a close friendship, one that had survived many crises. Lincoln, of course, had come out in favor of a lenient postwar policy toward the South before his assassination, and it was very likely that the new President, himself a southerner, expected Schurz to publicly support such a program now.

He could not have been more mistaken. Carl submitted a thorough and well-documented report, full of compassion for the newly liberated slaves. It urged immediate action to assure the Negro's right to vote, work and study. But it was less than charitable toward southern whites, especially former slaveholders. It recommended, too, that Union troops remain in the former Confederate states to guard against racial conflict, a move guaranteed to bruise southern pride, already well-battered.

The Schurz report reflected the harsh attitude of men like Charles Sumner of Massachusetts and Thaddeus Stevens of Vermont—Radical Republicans both—who wanted to keep a tight economic and legislative hold on the South. Stevens even insisted that "the proud traitors of the South" be humbled and that their states be treated as conquered provinces. It is doubtful if Schurz shared in this vengefulness; indeed, he was to change his position before long. But for the time being, his opinion on reconstruction put him squarely in Johnson's enemy camp. The report was received by the President with coolness, if not downright hostility, and set off a bitter feud between these two strong-minded men.

Thus rebuffed, Schurz accepted a bid from Horace Greeley to become Washington correspondent for the New York *Tribune,* a job he enjoyed tremendously, since it gave him unlimited opportunities to take pot shots at Johnson, whom he publicly described as "a very narrow man, obstinate and stubborn . . . a born demagogue."

Next spring brought another editorial offer, this one from the Detroit *Post.* Carl made the change with Greeley's blessings. Washington, after all, was only a telegraph key away. The attacks on the Johnson administration would continue.

Detroit in 1866 was a city of some 75,000, hardly the bustling manufacturing center it was to become within half a century, thanks to the genius of Henry Ford, born the year Carl Schurz led Union troops in the battle of Gettysburg. It had a large German population and a vocal liberal core.

When the drums started beating for the congressional elections that year, editor Schurz joined in eagerly, taking the stump in behalf of Radical Republicans everywhere. He could no more ignore politics than a terrier could a dog fight.

The embattled Andy Johnson fought back. His strategy was simple—put as many Democrats in Congress as possible and thus push through a favorable reconstruction policy for the South. The Republican battle plan was equally deliberate—load both houses with *their* men so that Johnson's hands, in effect, would be tied.

The election results of 1866 pleased Schurz enormously. Forty-two Republicans were voted to the Senate as against 11 Democrats. The margin was nearly as great in the House of Representatives, 143 to 49. "Well, we have succeeded in mastering Johnson at the right moment," Schurz wrote complacently in his daily column of opinion. "During the rest of his administration Congress will rule without paying much attention to him."

Clearly, this was a case of wishful thinking. Whatever faults old "Andy" may have had—he was known to be crude, short-tempered, and loud—giving up easily was not one of them. Sizing up the odds, he now began to pick off his enemies one by one. Congress immediately countered by passing the Tenure of Office Act, which forbade the President from removing anyone in office without the express consent of the Senate. Then, when a fighting-mad Johnson challenged the act by deliberately firing his Secretary of State, William Stanton, the battle was joined. The result was the historical impeachment assault against Andrew Johnson, the first time any President of the United States had ever been brought to trial during his term of office.

Carl Schurz played a unique role in this crisis, which came

to a head in March, 1868. Before then, however, he was to face a few crises of his own.

First, he changed jobs again when the St. Louis *Westliche Post,* one of the leading German-language newspapers in the country, made him a fine offer—an editorship together with a half interest in the paper. He jumped at the opportunity, even though he knew it might have been more comfortable to return to Watertown where his mother and father still lived in the large farmhouse that had been Carl's first real home in America. His two sisters, meantime, had long since married and left the Schurz homestead.

After a quick visit with his aging parents in Watertown, Carl became convinced that his future would be shaped by opportunities that presented themselves, such as the St. Louis offer, rather than by ties to the past. Certainly Watertown was an attractive community; life would be much easier there than in the hurly-burly of St. Louis, especially for Margarethe. But the challenge lay beyond the lovely hills of southern Wisconsin, and there Carl Schurz followed his destiny.

No sooner had the family moved to St. Louis, however, than tragedy struck. Emma Savannah, barely two years old, died after a brief illness. Carl was grief-stricken, but the burden on his wife was almost too much for her to bear. He therefore decided that she and the two girls—Agatha was then fourteen, Marianne eleven—had best go to Germany for a while.

"Perhaps the clear air of the Rhineland will restore your health and heart," he murmured to Margarethe.

"Perhaps," was her bereaved response.

Carl then settled down to a busy bachelor's life, moving in with Dr. Emil Pretorius, chief editor of the *Westliche Post* and himself a Radical Republican who threw the entire weight of his German language newspaper into the political arena. All through that long and hot St. Louis summer, Schurz dipped his pen in venom and hurled it at Andrew Johnson.

But not all of Carl's words were destructive. He wrote many thoughtful editorials and speeches on state and federal responsibilities, on the advantages of free trade, the need for conservation of natural resources. Responsible party leaders began to take notice of the St. Louis editor. "Now there's a man who'd make a mighty fine Senator from Missouri," they began to whisper to one another. If Schurz heard these remarks he did nothing to discourage them. He too had set his sights beyond his ink-stained editor's desk.

Just before Christmas of 1867, he took a long-delayed vacation and booked passage to Germany in order to join his family. However, he set foot on his native land with some apprehension. Would the German government, now under Chancellor Bismarck, clap him in jail because of his revolutionary past?

Much to his surprise, Carl was greeted with warmth and respect wherever he went. His record as a distinguished political figure from the New World had preceded him. The autocratic Bismarck even granted him a private interview in which he subtly suggested that Schurz return to Germany and enter the diplomatic service of his fatherland.

"You flatter me, Herr Chancellor," Carl replied over coffee and cigars. "But my life, and the future of my family, is committed to America." Happily, he had found Margarethe much improved and planned to return with her in a matter of weeks.

"You cannot blame me for trying," Bismarck sighed. "It was a stupid thing for Germany to have lost a talent like yours. By the by, Herr Schurz, I hear you are as adept at the piano as you are at politics. Is that so?" For the rest of the evening, statesmanship gave way to Chopin and Mozart. Carl thoroughly enjoyed playing the piano and always managed to spend a few hours at the instrument each week in spite of his busy schedule.

When Carl and his family returned to America in March, 1868, impeachment proceedings against President Johnson were under way. The House of Representatives had already condemned him; now the Senate had him on the rack. Editor Schurz hurried to Washington and took a seat in the press gallery.

Listening to the testimony, he began to question, for the first time, the validity of the case against Johnson as presented by Senator Ben Butler for the prosecution. The arguments, it seemed to him, were being put forward in a dull, dry fashion. Were the charges themselves equally dry, without real basis in fact? Carl wondered.

He also questioned some of the methods used by the prosecution, both during the trial and behind the scenes. From his vantage point as a journalist, he witnessed every unscrupulous tactic—smear, innuendo, character assassination. He saw it all and was disgusted by it. And he saw something else —the determination of a small group of Radical Republican senators who refused to be pressured or bribed into delivering a guilty verdict as demanded by the party leadership. There were seven men in this group, seven who placed principle above political expediency.

"I cannot indict on the facts before me," insisted Senator John B. Henderson, of Missouri.

"Indict or face the loss of party support!" thundered Ben Butler in the privacy of his own chambers.

"I cannot indict on the facts before me," repeated Henderson during the public trial.

So it went with the other six, incorruptible to the end. All were fully aware that their political careers were now finished as far as the party was concerned.

When the verdict was finally handed down on May 16, 1868, the much-maligned Johnson was acquitted by the margin of a single vote! The seven senators who had refused to indict under pressure had tipped the scales!

Carl studied the victory of reason over passion. Though he still had no love for Johnson, he came to the reluctant conclusion that perhaps the man was more sinned against than sinning. Later, in his own memoirs, he wrote that the impeachment effort had been a great mistake and that "good citizens had permitted themselves to be taken off their feet" in the pursuit of vengeance. He also praised the band of faithful senators who "maintained their convictions of right and justice" in the face of political suicide.

Johnson's impeachment trial had an important bearing on Schurz's career. First, it was a forcible reminder that truth must always be placed above expediency. Second, it opened the door for his next political move—the active pursuit of a Senate seat from Missouri. Ironically, this was made possible by the incumbent John Henderson himself, who, when his term of office expired at the end of 1868, failed to win his party's support because of his pro-Johnson stand.

By then, Carl Schurz had been thrust even further into the political limelight. Appointed a delegate-at-large from Missouri to the Republican National Convention in the summer of 1868, he was named temporary chairman, a significant honor. He also wrote into the party platform a more compassionate policy toward the South, further evidence that he had lost much of his old harshness.

The convention that year nominated General Ulysses S. Grant for the Presidency, a choice with which Schurz heartily agreed. The Democrats, meantime, nominated Horatio Seymour, little known then and even less so after his ignoble defeat at the hands of the colorful and popular Grant. With the presidential contest decided, Schurz turned his attention to the Senate race.

In those days, United States senators were elected by members of state legislatures rather than by popular vote, as is the case today; frequently the vote was taken before or after the national elections themselves. The change to the popular vote for senatorial candidates was put into effect by the Seventeenth Amendment to the Constitution, passed in 1912. Under the system as it existed before then, however, choice of senators was often prearranged by party bosses, and the state legislators frequently went along. This was very much the case in Missouri until Carl Schurz stepped into the picture.

The leading candidate up to that time was Benjamin Loan, of St. Joseph, the personal choice of Charles Drake, the senior senator from Missouri who also held the Republican reins in the state. His consternation knew no bounds when Schurz announced for the candidacy. As Loan's campaign manager, Drake denounced the upstart editor as a "Heinie" infidel, a professional revolutionary and a coward. Newspaper accounts testify that the campaign, as waged up and down the state, was one of the most vicious on record.

However, candidate Schurz stuck to his guns. He fired back salvo after salvo, trying whenever possible to stick to issues rather than personalities. Forty-eight newspapers in Missouri supported the more articulate Schurz, including the *Westliche Post* and the St. Louis *Democrat,* while only thirteen favored Loan.

The campaign rose to fever pitch just before Christmas. "My life is a continuous battle," Carl protested to his wife one night, after a particularly trying speaking tour. "I don't see any end to it for as long as I remain in politics."

Margarethe poured him another cup of coffee. "You sound so sad, as though fighting for what you believe were something new."

"Not new, Margarethe. Just more difficult. Remember, I will be forty years old next March. The fires no longer burn as brightly." He sighed wearily, then picked up his pen. There was, after all, tomorrow's editorial to write.

"Perhaps not as brightly," Margarethe agreed, "but with more heat." Then she closed the door, leaving him to his own thoughts.

The Missouri legislators met in Jefferson City, the capital, on January 6, 1869, to cast ballots for the open Senatorial seat from their state. Both candidates and their campaign managers—Colonel Grosvenor, editor of the St. Louis *Democrat,* served Schurz in that capacity—circulated among the lawmakers, each doing his best to impress. Up to now, Carl had without success been trying to debate with Loan face to face. But Charles Drake, wily and full of intrigue, had always managed to steer his less colorful candidate away from a confrontation.

Schurz's opportunity finally came during a smoke-filled reception in a crowded hotel room, two days before the balloting. "My man," Schurz heard Drake loudly proclaim, "will push for more federal funds for his native state. Send him to the Senate, gentlemen, and Missouri will not want for appropriations!"

"Not very likely!" Carl stepped up and confronted Drake, at the same time fixing an eye on Benjamin Loan, who stood abjectly at the senior senator's side. "First-term senators never sit on important committees, not unless they've had previous experience in government." Now he turned confidently to his listeners. "May I remind this distinguished gathering that I served that great Republican, Abraham Lincoln, as his Ambassador to Spain." He was not above using hyperbole when it suited the occasion.

Schurz had scored and Drake knew it. "Served as a political hack!" he suddenly exploded.

Carl drew himself up to his full height, the tallest man in the room. "I dare you, sir," he taunted, "to repeat that charge in public debate. And without your congressional immunity!"

Drake swallowed the bait. "Whenever and wherever you wish, *Herr* Schurz!" He emphasized the German word with some distaste.

"At *your* convenience, *Mister* Drake!" The barb hit home as Carl knew it would, since politicians resent not being called by their official titles.

Word of the feud spread, and a packed audience gathered at the town hall the next evening. Benjamin Loan spoke first with little distinction, after which Senator Drake took the stand. A far more effective speaker, he soon had the crowd bending his way. He played with his listeners, leading them about like so many sheep, so much so that he soon became overconfident. "I leave it to you," he shouted hoarsely at the peak of his delivery, "whether or not you wish to be represented in Washington by a man who might sooner serve fellow Germans rather than native-born Americans!"

This insult was too much, even for a crowd that had come to see political blood flow. They began to hoot Drake and stamp their feet, then shouted for Schurz to take the stand.

Carl strode forward, smiling and alert. In a brilliant extemporaneous talk based on Drake's unfortunate attack, he made a strong case for German-American loyalty. "Indeed, I can say the same for anyone who came to America for the purpose of taking up citizenship in this country. Would any of us, though our ancestry be rooted in other lands, dare to take our citizenship lightly . . . say as lightly as Mr. Drake, who now questions our devotion to our adopted country?" Carl had rightly guessed that the room was well represented by those only a generation removed from their European roots.

Schurz had been through the mill before a hundred different audiences. A veteran of the speaking platform, he knew how to turn an apparent thrust to his own favor.

At midnight caucus that very evening, the legislators voted unanimously to send Carl Schurz to Washington as the other United States senator from Missouri.

8.

On March 4, 1869, just two days before his fortieth birthday, Carl Schurz walked down the center aisle of the United States Senate and took the oath of office as the junior senator from Missouri. Moments later, he joined the solemn procession that passed through the rotunda of the Capitol and out to the east steps where he saw Supreme Court Chief Justice Salmon P. Chase administer the presidential oath to Ulysses S. Grant as the eighteenth President of the United States.

Thus began the senatorial career of Carl Schurz. It lasted only one six-year term, until 1875. But it was a term full of storm and stress and conflicts over issues which separated dedicated statesmen from mere politicians.

He had come to Washington without promises to anyone but himself. "I recorded a vow in my heart," he later wrote in his memoirs, "that I would at least endeavor to fulfill that duty; and that I would conscientiously adhere to the principle *salus populi suprema lex*—the well-being of the people is the highest law—that I would never be a sycophant of power nor a flatterer of the multitude; that, if need be, I would stand up alone for my conviction of truth and right; and that there would be no personal sacrifice too great for my devotion to the Republic."

Schurz had many opportunities to flatter and be servile and to knuckle under to the dictates of the Grant administration, tactics which undoubtedly would have prolonged his senatorial career. But his political integrity had come fully of age by now. From here on in, he was to be his own man, regardless of the consequences.

His self-assurance on the Senate floor and his keen knowledge of world affairs soon won him a place on the important Foreign Relations Committee headed by Charles Sumner, a great honor for a first-year legislator. He was also appointed to three other Senate committees: Military Affairs, Pensions, and Territories. To each he brought his distinctive mark. However, in his driving passion for reform, Carl Schurz made as many enemies as friends.

Take, for example, the matter of civil service—the non-elective job system necessary to run the federal government and its many agencies. Carl had already been introduced to the spoils system many years ago by his friend Francis Grund, the newspaperman who was among the first to welcome him back to Washington. The freshman Senator was shocked anew by the waves of office-seekers that descended on the nation's capital with the change from Johnson to Grant.

"The patronage system is worse than ever," Grund pointed out. "But perhaps you can do something about it now, Carl." Schurz started to work on the problem at once.

He learned, first of all, that a certain Thomas Jenckes, congressman from Rhode Island, had introduced a civil service reform bill four years before only to have it swept aside by cynical lawmakers. Carl studied the main points of the Jenckes bill, then delivered a strong speech before the Senate—his "maiden" effort in the Upper House—in which he urged that the Tenure of Office Act *not* be repealed, as President Grant had urged, until a suitable civil service reform bill could be worked out. It was a daring stand. He hadn't yet learned that freshmen senators just didn't go against presidential wishes! Although Carl's motion won floor approval, it aroused Grant's scowling suspicions. "Keep that Missouri gadfly in his place," he growled at Oliver Morton, of Indiana, the Senate "whip," or floor leader. "I smell trouble from that direction."

Trouble or not, the "Missouri gadfly" was eventually appointed to Congress' Joint Committee on Retrenchment, which concerned itself, among other matters, with civil service. He was too much the legislative workhorse to be kept off so valuable an assignment.

Schurz immediately drew up a detailed civil service reform bill of his own. Briefly, it provided for an examining board to pass on candidates' qualifications, a year of probation for new jobholders and lengthening job tenure beyond the presidential term. It even suggested a salary scale for certain key posts. A year later, two bills were placed before Congress: the Schurz bill and one drawn up by Lyman Trumbull, the veteran senator from Illinois. The Senate preferred the Trumbull version, and the measure was eventually passed in 1872, with many of the features originally proposed by Schurz.

Even so, the bill had little effect. Much to Carl's disgust, the practical politicians who surrounded Grant had no intention of letting patronage slip from their greedy fingers. They treated the Trumbull Bill as if it were no more than a scrap of paper and continued to dole out government jobs. Obviously, they believed that "to the victors belong the spoils."

The President's indifference to rules disturbed Schurz deeply. One action in particular shook his confidence in him —the "Black Friday" panics of 1869.

That summer Jay Gould and James Fisk, Jr., two New York financiers, conspired to corner the market in gold bullion, so necessary for the conduct of foreign trade. In this bold maneuver, they hoped to get the help of President Grant's brother-in-law, who was supposed to use his influence to keep the government from interfering. The plan very nearly succeeded. Gould and Fisk bought up all the gold they could get their hands on. The price of the precious metal soared as available supplies diminished. Traders, desperate for gold exchange, paid premium prices to Gould and Fisk. The sudden drain on money and credit caused a series of financial panics that usually occurred on the last day of the trading week, therefore the term "Black Friday."

Finally, with traders on the verge of bankruptcy, Secretary of Treasury Boutwell ordered a sale of bullion from the government's own deposits. The plot to corner gold collapsed almost at once.

Although it was never proven that Grant himself was directly implicated, it was obvious to Carl Schurz and others that some of the President's friends and advisers were mixed up in the conspiracy.

"I wonder," the junior senator from Missouri confided afterward to Charles Sumner, by now his friend and political ally, "if we shouldn't keep an eye on the White House."

"At least one," Sumner agreed.

The breach between Schurz and Grant widened further with the Santo Domingo affair which came to a head late in 1870. The conflict was clear-cut. President Grant wanted to annex the Caribbean Island kingdom, later known as the Dominican Republic, to the United States. Carl Schurz opposed the action.

"Under no circumstances," he firmly debated, "should this

nation grant statehood to a territory so far from the mainland." In this he was seconded by Chairman Sumner and a majority of the Foreign Relations Committee.

But Grant persisted. He even sent an official to Santo Domingo to explore the matter further. His emissary did more than that; he drew up treaties that would, in effect, have annexed the island territory to the United States.

When the bill finally reached the Senate floor, Sumner and Schurz voted against it, as did twenty-six other senators, thus killing the measure. Grant, of course, was furious. His first act of vengeance was to ask for the resignation of Charles Sumner's close friend, John Motley, as Ambassador to England. His second act was to treat Carl Schurz as though he did not exist.

But Carl did, much to the President's chagrin.

They crossed legislative paths again, this time over the question of trade. A free trader, Schurz supported lower tariffs and had joined with William Cullen Bryant and others to form the American Free Trade League in 1869. When, in 1870, the Grant administration pushed for a restrictive trade bill, Carl bolted party lines again.

An angry Grant placed a red check mark against the name of the junior senator from Missouri. "I mean to exterminate this man's influence," he vowed, "one way or the other!"

Grant's opportunity came over the issue of southern reconstruction. As a former Confederate state, Missouri had many political restrictions placed against it. But now, more than five years after the Civil War, Carl Schurz felt it was time to lift them. "The administration must forgive and forget," he said at the Missouri state convention held in the fall of 1870. "The right to vote and hold office must be granted to every peaceful citizen of Missouri."

But the regular Republicans who controlled the state

party were of another mind. They rebuffed all attempts to amend the state constitution. Carl Schurz was convinced he could no longer work within the party organization, especially in Missouri. "If we want to win our case, we'd better make our move now," he confided to close political friends.

Much to his satisfaction, some 250 liberal-minded delegates shared his views. The Schurz-led dissidents organized their own convention and nominated their own candidates. The resulting commotion was heard all the way to Washington. "Confound it!" roared Grant. "I thought I gave orders to exterminate that gadfly!"

The administration tried. Money poured into Missouri for the express purpose of defeating the dissident ticket. Pressure was brought to bear on all federal officeholders in that state to support regular Republican candidates. The going was rough for the liberals. Schurz admitted at the time that "Grant has read me out of the party and is vigorously at work chopping off the official heads of those suspected of sympathizing with me."

In spite of White House interference, the Schurz forces were swept into office, and the Missouri state constitution was amended so as to give former Confederate sympathizers the right to vote. When Congress reconvened in Washington later that year, Schurz found himself *persona non grata* at the White House. The President had left word that he was no longer at home to the junior senator from Missouri.

Schurz's promise that he "would stand up alone for my convictions of truth and right" had already cost him presidential favor.

Later, defending himself before a hushed Senate, he explained his independent stand. "I recognize objects in political life superior to the immediate advantages of party. I have never been able to look up to a political organization as a deity. . . ." Then leveling his gaze at Republican leaders

Morton and Conkling, Schurz cut the cord that tied him to his party. "Nor do I regard the possibility of organizing a new party as anything criminal!" A brave statement to make, but as far as the regular Republicans were concerned, a heretical one!

In all this turmoil, Carl found time to be a good husband and father. Nothing pleased him more than to spend a quiet evening at his Washington home with his wife and two children. He also enjoyed the piano; Bach and Beethoven revived him, especially after a grueling day in the Senate.

It was here in the nation's capital that Margarethe gave birth to their third child and first son early in 1871. The elated couple named him Carl, after his distinguished father.

Carl Schurz was deeply moved when his independent position drew friends to his side. "How can we help?" they asked eagerly.

"Form a third force strong enough to defeat Grant next year," he promptly responded. Something like that had been on his mind for some time. Now that he saw he had allies from both sides of the political fence, he went to work in earnest. He drew up a tentative platform for the "new wave" in national politics: general amnesty to southerners, self-rule for former Confederate states (northern armies were still stationed below the Mason-Dixon line), civil service reform, reduction of tariffs, a return to sound money, and more effective control of big business. In between congressional sessions, he toured the nation, spreading his gospel of reform.

Carl received powerful support from the press. Horace Greeley of the New York *Tribune,* called the Missouri senator a "great political missionary, laboring for the defeat of Grant." More help came from Murat Halstead of the Cincinnati *Commercial,* and from Horace White of the Chicago

Tribune. The Springfield (Illinois) *Republican* and the *Nation* also supported him.

The insurgent movement gained momentum and finally broke out in the open late in January, 1872. The Liberal (formerly Radical) Republicans of Missouri electrified the political world by calling for a national convention of third-party forces to be held May 1 in Cincinnati. Schurz was overjoyed.

Meanwhile, help of a sort came from another source, though at first Carl called it a liability. It took the form of political attacks on him from Thomas Nast, one of the great cartoonists of the nineteenth century.

With his powerful pen, Nast had just helped put Tammany's corrupt Boss Tweed behind bars. He now looked about for another target and settled on Carl Schurz and his third-party force. Nast may have felt obligated to the regular Republican party which had fought so valiantly for Tweed's conviction in New York. If the Republicans were now fighting Schurz, so would he. By a strange coincidence, both men were German-Americans, the younger Nast having been born in Landau, some eleven years after Schurz. Stranger still, the cartoonist later was to become an admirer of Schurz and to draw him in a far different light. But at the time, he was merciless in his attacks.

At first, Carl was furious about the caricatures. He thought it treasonable for one German-American to attack another or, for that matter, to poke fun at any group or individual fighting Grant's corrupt administration. Appropriately enough, Schurz presented a tempting figure for the artist, with his tall frame, sharp features, bushy beard and flashing eyes.

"Look at this!" the Missouri senator fumed, slapping a Nast cartoon depicting him as a cunning devil trying to arouse a figure (Sumner's) to carry a legislative spear against Grant. "What is Nast trying to do, ruin me?"

Francis Grund, his old newspaper friend, shook his head. "On the contrary. He may be doing you a favor."

Carl looked at him in surprise. "By sticking an editorial knife in my back?"

"By giving you national publicity," Grund replied, "Nast is helping spread the name and face of Carl Schurz across the country. Sure, he may not be very flattering, drawing you as a Mephistopheles or a Don Quixote, but he is doing more for your reform program than a hundred speeches or a dozen editorials. One picture—"

"Is worth a thousand words!" Carl finished the old adage with a slow smile. "I see what you mean. Though I would ask a little more kindness from such a clever man."

Among people who knew Schurz, the caricatures did no harm. Among those who didn't, Nast's drawings only served to make them ask, "Who is this man Schurz, anyway? And what does he stand for?" When they took the trouble to find out, they invariably became more sympathetic to his cause.

Thomas Nast was to have a lasting effect on political life in the United States. He originated the cartoon symbols of the Democratic donkey and the Republican elephant, though neither was intended to stand for what it does today. In 1870, Nast drew the donkey—or jackass, as he inelegantly described it—to attack certain editors and newspapers favoring the Democrats. It became such a popular figure that soon he and other cartoonists were using the donkey as the symbol for all Democrats.

The same was true of the elephant, which Nast sketched in 1874, not to symbolize the Republicans but to denote the huge vote rolled up by their party. In time, the elephant, too, became the symbol of the party itself.

9. Where the eagle flies, the vulture follows close behind.

Carl Schurz should have been familiar with this frontier axiom. But the leader of the Liberal Republicans paid little attention to the political vultures that flocked to the third-party convention which began on May 1, 1872, in Cincinnati. His only concern then was to choose the best possible presidential candidate to run against Grant in November. Nothing else mattered.

Carl's personal choice was the wise and cultured Charles Francis Adams, son of John Quincy Adams, the sixth President of the United States. "Adams will lead us in the good fight," Senator Schurz assured his friends. Political amateurs for the most part, they agreed, unaware of the hostile maneuverings going on behind their back.

A hidden war against the Schurz faction was under way even before the convention began, led by Frank Blair, Jr., the shrewd Democratic senator from Missouri. A party hack, Blair had been thrust into office only the year before. He had no use for Schurz and his liberal group; his chief aim was to get the highest possible post for his own man, Missouri Governor G. Gratz Brown, who had, ironically enough, been elected to that post only because Schurz had had the courage to fight the regular Republicans in his home state two years before.

Other unscrupulous "birds of a feather" flocked to Cincinnati for different reasons. Some were hungry for office; some were sent there to rip and tear away at the Liberal Republicans; a few peddled their votes to the highest bidder. True, they made up only a small proportion of the delegates, most of whom were honest and decent folk. But once they had a rallying point—and Blair saw to it that one was established behind the scenes—they began to exert an influence far beyond their numbers.

A more sophisticated liberal leadership should have deployed at once. But Schurz had little taste for political infighting, which he felt beneath his dignity. His foes, however, had no such scruples and began to pull out the eagle's talons one by one.

Blair's first tactic was to get Schurz, the acknowledged convention leader, off the floor. This he accomplished by having one of his secret spokesmen to nominate Schurz as convention chairman, a move that was quickly seconded and unanimously approved by a wildly cheering crowd. Carl was greatly stirred by the honor and delivered a moving speech in support of the liberals' lofty aims.

Far back in the galleries, lost in the shadows, a calculating Blair measured the crowd's reaction. "It's a good thing," he whispered to an aide, "that that Dutchman was born in Germany. Otherwise he'd win the presidential nomination hands down."

As chairman, Schurz moved the meeting along briskly enough. But when political maneuvering began, he saw, too late, that his skill and energy were needed more on the floor as a leader than on the platform as chairman. He found himself chained to the rostrum, unable to take sides, unable to counter the opposition's clever moves. Instead of leading arguments in favor of Charles Francis Adams, Carl helplessly pounded the gavel for order. Blair, still in the background, had scored his first important victory.

With Schurz neutralized, the politicians retreated to their smoke-filled rooms to map their next move. Their strategy was simple: stop the nomination of a strong Liberal Republican. The White House, after all, was the biggest political plum in the country. It was not likely they would have a share in it if someone like Adams got in, especially with a sharp-eyed Schurz hovering in the background.

To be sure, they weren't without opposition for long. As soon as word got around that Blair was on the premises, a group of liberal newspaper editors, among them Carl Schurz, planned their own counter-strategy. But these were honorable men. They insisted their high ideals were enough to see them through.

"We must not stoop to their low level!" Carl urged. "I am confident that we can win without adopting the very means we are sworn to defeat!"

Meantime, the convention had settled on four men as presidential possibilities—Charles Francis Adams, Senator Lyman Trumbull of Illinois, Horace Greeley, and Blair's own handpicked candidate, G. Gratz Brown.

The first ballot cheered Chairman Schurz. Adams ran up 205 votes against Greeley's 147, with Trumbull and Brown bringing up the rear. Good, but not good enough. Carl thought perhaps Adams could widen his lead in the second ballot.

Adams did, but not by enough to start a trend. Also, the little-known name of G. Gratz Brown hung on in the balloting, much to the chairman's surprise. What Carl could not know was that all week long Blair had been showering favors on delegates, most of whom had never before been exposed to politicking. If a labor group from Chicago called for beer,

Blair bought them beer, by the barrels. If New Yorkers called for champagne, he ordered champagne. Food and cigars popped up everywhere, and even gifts for the delegates, sent with the "best wishes of Senator Blair, who has only the best wishes of the public at heart."

His pressure tactics became more obvious as the convention approached its climax. Blair organized squads of burly men who blocked off opposing floor speakers from the chairman's view. His thugs set off firecrackers or started fights in the galleries when it suited him. Or paid claques cheered the name of G. Gratz Brown and hooted at every mention of Charles Francis Adams or Lyman Trumbull, liberals both.

In spite of diversions, the balloting continued. At the end of the third round, Adams still held a narrow lead. "If only one of the other candidates would withdraw!" Schurz confided to friends.

While Schurz was hoping for a break, Blair was planning one. He had conceded by now that his man Brown could never sweep the delegates. His next move was to push for the nomination of a pliable candidate, one whom he could control—perhaps Horace Greeley. The *Tribune* editor looked better by the hour. To the crafty Senator, anyone was preferable to Adams or Trumbull. Also, the gullible Greeley might just be talked into accepting Brown as his running mate—*if* the latter got him the nomination.

Greeley couldn't be bribed, of that Blair was certain, but he surely could be manipulated. As the Senator prepared to do just that, Schurz began to prepare for the fourth ballot.

"Order! The chair calls for order!" Chairman Schurz banged the gavel. After repeated entreaties, the delegates slumped into their chairs, fanning themselves into silence. It could be hot in Cincinnati, even in May.

Frank Blair sprang into action at that precise moment of

suspended silence. With a quick shove he sent the rotund figure of G. Gratz Brown out into a cleared aisle. At another signal, a leather-lunged delegate addressed himself to the chair. "I move for a special statement by the honorable candidate from Missouri!"

Schurz cut him short with a rap of the gavel. "Out of order! The delegate on the floor"—he pointed in the direction of the interruption—"is out of order!"

"But Mr. Chairman—!"

"The chair now calls for a fourth ballot!"

Governor Brown, hurrying toward the platform, added his voice to the commotion. Delegates began to sit up with new interest. A floor fight! "The candidate from Missouri," the onrushing Brown pleaded, "begs to be recognized for an important—"

Carl fairly splintered the rostrum with another blow. "Mr. Brown, you know full well no nominee may make a statement once balloting begins. Those are the rules—"

G. Gratz Brown looked up, his eyes blinking in innocence. "But the voting hasn't begun!"

"Then I hereby open the roll," Carl announced, "by calling on the delegation from Alabama!"

He was interrupted by another loud voice from the floor. "Give the man a chance why don't you?"

"Yeah!" another chimed in, right on cue. "You afraid of what he has to say?"

Exasperated, Schurz tried to regain control. "Order! Order!"

The shouts from the floor drowned him out. "Let the man speak!"

"Speech! Speech!"

" 'Ray for free speech!"

The gavel rapped in vain. Shouts for "freedom of speech,"

organized at first by Blair's claque, soon spread through the hall. Carl tried to stem the rising clamor, then fearful that the convention might turn to riot, reluctantly pointed to G. Gratz Brown. "The chair," he intoned, "temporarily suspends balloting and recognizes the candidate from Missouri. But only for two minutes!"

The audience yelped at the byplay, eager for something to break the monotony of roll calls. They continued cheering as the squat, triumphant Brown strutted up the four steps of the platform and posed in back of the speaker's stand. When he raised his short arms, the delegates quickly subsided into an expectant hush.

The governor from Missouri was a born spellbinder. "Unity," he began, "is the most urgent business of this convention!" The crowd roared in approval. "Only if we stand behind *one* man can our voices be heard all the way to Washington and reach every independent voter in this glorious *United* States!" More howls of agreement. "Delegates from near and far"—he leaned his impassioned face over the speaker's stand—"in the name of unity, I therefore withdraw my own name in favor of—" His eyes swept the galleries; the dramatic pause sent an expectant thrill through the packed hall "—in favor of the one man who can lead us to victory . . . Horace Greeley, the sage from Chappaqua, New York!"

The answering roars tumbled over the rows of seats, washed up against the platform, engulfed the hall. Dumbfounded, Schurz pounded for order, but he might as well have been in the next county. The emotional dam had burst. Within moments it had carried Horace Greeley, perhaps the most startled man at the convention, to victory as the near unanimous choice of the Liberal Republicans. Greeley's grateful response was all that Frank Blair could have hoped: he selected G. Gratz Brown, the man who had supposedly started the Greeley bandwagon rolling, as his vice-presidential running mate.

Liberal leaders that night gathered in the depressed atmosphere of Carl Schurz's hotel suite where they glumly listened to their erstwhile chairman improvising at the piano. "They stole it," he murmured over and over again. "They stole the convention right out from under our noses! Political robbery in broad daylight!" Then a harsh chord ended the soliloquy. "Gentlemen!" Carl turned toward his friends. "The sad truth is that we have been enslaved by the very monsters we started out to destroy!"

The presidential campaign of 1872, like so many others before and since, was called by observers "the dirtiest on record." Historical facts bear out this familiar description. Arguments over issues gave way to arguments over personalities. Fingers pointed, tempers flared, voices were raised in anger.

"Drunken sot!" Greeley supporters jibed at Grant.

"Mother hen!" the President's backers railed at Greeley. "And Schurz, the crowing rooster!"

Despite his disgust at the outcome of the convention, Carl could not stay out of a fight against Grant. He became one of Greeley's closest advisers, a relationship which Thomas Nast exploited without mercy. The cartoonist drew contemptuous caricatures of the lanky Schurz ministering to a moon-faced, chin-whiskered Horace Greeley, complete with top hat and long white coat, the editor's characteristic garb. Meanwhile, brickbats continued to fly.

Schurz caught his share of mud-slinging. "Foreign mercenary!" was the mildest epithet leveled at him. Impervious to name-calling, he took the abuse in stride. But the mild-mannered Greeley, a Quaker, winced at the charges. "Sometimes I wonder whether I'm running for the presidency or the penitentiary!" he wailed.

The election was almost anticlimactic. Even though Greeley also gained the support of the Democrats that year, he took only six of the thirty-six states which then made up the Union. Grant won by a landslide, burying the Liberal Republicans and their Democratic allies under a barrage of ballots.

Ironically, had the sage from Chappaqua been elected, he would never have assumed office. Horace Greeley died of brain fever three weeks after his defeat, a tired, spent and disillusioned man.

10. Carl Schurz was just about the loneliest man on Capitol Hill when Congress reconvened in December, 1872. His role with the Liberal Republicans had made him even more of an administration outcast than before. Many of his Senate colleagues avoided him, lest some of the Schurz brand of independence rub off on them. He was snubbed in the cloakroom, ignored in the Senate restaurant and seldom asked out to dinner parties except by a few close friends such as Charles Sumner and Lyman Trumbull.

This didn't bother Carl much. What hurt more was his loss of legislative assignments; he was dropped from all committee posts but one, that on the Senate Foreign Relations Committee.

A lesser man might have retreated, content to ride out the privileged sanctuary of high office. But Schurz was no ordinary man. He threw himself headlong into legislative work still open to him and continued to press for civil service reform in hopes that someone would ask his help in the matter. The call never came—not then, at any rate.

With more time on his hands, Carl turned once more to his pen. He expanded his memoirs and updated his speeches. He wrote vivid dispatches for the St. Louis *Westliche Post,* where he still retained the editorship. And he began to take preliminary notes on a biography of Henry Clay, whom he admired as a great American statesman of the recent past.

Best of all, he was able to spend more time with his family. The infant Carl, born the year before, was a constant joy to the parents. Marianne, at sixteen, was busy with school. But it was Agatha, a comely and intelligent young lady approaching her twentieth birthday, who was the apple of her father's eye.

Carl had good reason to admire her. She did much of his basic research and copied his speeches and editorials in a strong, clear hand. She kept his voluminous files in order and became an expert secretary.

But admiration for Agatha was also mixed with concern. "Shouldn't you worry less about your father's work, young lady, and more about getting out in the world? I see some very eligible young bachelors on Capitol Hill, especially in the law libraries, to say nothing of receptions and teas. Now promise me next time we're invited, you'll put on your prettiest frock."

Agatha gave him a quick smile. "I promise, Father. Now, did you want any more on the Supreme Court decisions concerning the railroads?"

"Not for today, Agatha." He pushed himself away from his cluttered desk. "Let's treat ourselves to the theater tonight, shall we? They say Edwin Thomas Booth's *Hamlet* is something not to be missed."

Content with work and family, Schurz wrote in his journal that "he who walks his path with unswerving fidelity to his conviction of right has nothing to fear." Loneliness for him thus became a position of advantage from where he looked down on a frenetic society.

Inwardly he was less calm. Events in Washington bore out his worst fears of what he called "Grantism." Corruption in government became commonplace, and there was scarcely a month when some high official did not resign because of malfeasance in office.

History is witness to the times.

A number of congressmen and administration officials were found to have taken bribes from the Crédit Mobilier, the private corporation formed to finance the construction of the Union Pacific Railroad.

The President's own secretary was implicated in the infamous "Whiskey Ring" which defrauded the Internal Revenue Bureau of millions of tax dollars.

Grant's Secretary of War, William Belknap, was caught selling Indian post traderships and resigned under a cloud.

Further investigation revealed that his Secretary of the Navy, George M. Robeson, had piled up a personal fortune through illegal kickbacks on business contracts.

More than one observer called this the gilded age of money-grabbing and influence-peddling. Mark Twain took a close look at Washington, then wrote a novel in 1873, appropriately entitled *The Gilded Age,* in which he described the nation's capital as a city where "every individual you encounter . . . represents political influence. Mere merit, fitness, and capability are useless baggage without influence. . . ." Schurz had used these very sentiments in his fight for civil service reform!

There is no record that these two men from Missouri—Mark Twain was born in Hannibal in 1835—ever met at this time. However, they did meet later and became good friends. Neither man was pretentious; both attacked hypocrisy, Schurz in political life, Twain in social life.

One direct result of what Schurz called "Grantism" was the business panic of 1873. Once the public got wind of the administration's free and easy policies, it lost confidence in financial institutions. They withdrew money from banks and bought only bare necessities. As a consequence, the huge banking empire of Jay Cooke and Company closed its doors; other banks followed suit. Factories shut down, unemployment spread. The panic was on!

Money became scarce. An immediate clamor arose for cheap currency—greenbacks printed without regard to gold backing—especially among farmers and working people. Schurz sounded a stern warning. "If the administration bows to this senseless demand for inflated currency, it will doom the nation for generations to come!" He remained an advocate of sound money throughout his long career.

To Carl's vast relief, Grant refused to sign a runaway money bill, a stand which somewhat lessened the Missouri senator's criticism of the Chief Executive. As a matter of record, Schurz was more critical of the men surrounding the President than the President himself. He readily acknowledged that Grant had never knowingly engaged in questionable deals. However, it was the President's indiscreet choice of friends and White House aides that heaped abuse on his unfortunate head.

In subsequent accounts, Schurz clarified his appraisal of the eighteenth President of the United States. He conceded that Grant had swept many carpetbaggers out of the South and thus hastened reconstruction. He readily applauded the fact that he reduced the national debt; that he successfully settled America's suit against England through the Alabama Claims, which awarded the United States $15.5 million for damages inflicted on Northern shipping during the Civil War. But he never forgave the man for bringing to Washington those unscrupulous individuals who were able to "purchase with money their way to the highest legislative dignity of the greatest of Republics."

Carl's deep love for America was clearly evident in all he said and did. No man, in or out of government, ever had a higher regard for "the greatest of Republics," to use his own words.

Schurz's devotion to his country was demonstrated in his memorable response to Senator Matthew Carpenter of Wisconsin. The argument arose when Carl claimed that the United States had blundered in selling arms to France during the Franco-Prussian War of 1870–71. Carpenter immediately pounced on his fellow senator, charging him with a lack of patriotism. "Whatever happened to the cry of 'My country, right or wrong'?" he demanded.

At this point, Carl Schurz took the Senate floor, fixed an indignant eye on his accuser and declared for all to hear: "My country right or wrong, yes! If right, to be kept right; if wrong, to be *set* right!"

Schurz's regard for principle was dramatically revealed in another debate, this one with Senator Oliver Morton, the administration's sounding board. One day, when Schurz voted against a bill sponsored by the Republicans, Morton denounced him as "an inconsistent Republican." He had had just about enough of the Missouri senator's independence.

Carl replied to the charge with a ringing counterattack. "I want him [Morton] to point out in my record a single principle that I have ever betrayed. I want him to show where in the platforms of policy I have favored a single contradiction. He will not find one! *He* has never left his party. *I* have never betrayed my principles! That is the difference between him and me!"

The gallery cheered; the Democrats applauded. Morton

leaned back with a twisted smile. Brave talk from a foolish fellow! Obviously, Schurz had no interest in re-election, otherwise he would be much more cautious about flouting party loyalty.

A less prejudiced observer, historian James Ford Rhodes, had a far different view. In spite of the fact that Carl Schurz served only a single term in office, Rhodes called him "almost an ideal Senator."

Carl's term expired in March, 1875. He had long before decided that it would be futile to run for re-election. Opposed by a strong Democratic tide then sweeping the nation, ignored by the regular Republicans and supported only by a handful of reformers, he chose a dignified exit rather than ignominious defeat.

But if he thought he could leave the Senate without recognition from his many admirers, Carl was greatly, and happily, mistaken. In April of that year, he was tendered a surprise testimonial dinner in New York's fashionable Delmonico Restaurant. Two hundred distinguished guests were present —editors, educators, lawyers, businessmen, even congressmen from both sides of the aisle. All lauded the former senator for placing principle over party. The affair, said the New York *Tribune,* was the result of "the obvious desire of men of all parties to do honor to the statesman who had declared and maintained his independence. . . ."

Reporters besieged Schurz after the banquet. "What are your plans, Senator? Will you retire now? Or help your party? And have you made any promises?"

Schurz raised his hands in mock surprise. "Retire, gentlemen? Has my service in the Senate pushed me beyond my forty-six years? At that age, a man just begins to cut his political teeth . . . that is, if the opposition hasn't knocked them out by then. Now about helping my party . . . that all depends on the man the Republicans finally choose to run for President. As for promises, there's only one I've made since leaving office."

The ring of reporters raised their pads and pencils in anticipation.

"That was to Mrs. Schurz," Carl smiled again. "I promised her that after six stormy years in the Senate, the least I could do was to spend a peaceful year with her in Europe, on vacation!"

The entire family sailed for Europe the following month. But no sooner did they arrive in Germany than Margarethe's lungs began to bother her. She coughed incessantly, and the Schurzes, including the three children, spent most of their holiday near a sanitarium in the German Alps where Mrs. Schurz underwent treatment. In this unlikely place, Carl found himself involved in politics again, this time by remote control.

It began with a cable from America. "We need your help," Liberal Republicans pleaded. "Our cause at stake in Ohio. Please advise."

Carl might have been excused for begging off. He was on vacation; besides, his wife was ailing. But he knew the importance of Ohio where Rutherford Hayes, a moderate Republican, was running for Governor against William Allen, a veteran Democrat. It was a key election for the entire nation.

Debate in that particular campaign centered on sound money, overriding all local issues. Republican Hayes favored tight control of the dollar; Democrat Allen came out for the unlimited printing of greenbacks in hopes of getting the economy moving. Schurz rightly guessed, even from Europe, that the outcome in the Buckeye State could well set an example for the rest of the country.

At first he supported Hayes through the mails by writing long articles in his behalf for publication in America. "Not enough," his backers cabled back. "Hayes in danger. Voters, especially German element, want to hear you in person. Urge your immediate presence."

When Carl discussed the problem with Margarethe, she insisted on his return. "You'll be happier there, I know," she explained. "Go back and take Agatha with you. No, please," she waved off his protests. "You'll need her far more than I will. Marianne can take care of me, and it will only be for a little while, until I get well again." She coughed into a handkerchief. "Let me rest here at the sanitarium. Then in the spring, when I'm better, we'll rejoin you at home. I promise!"

Her physician convinced Carl that Margarethe would be better off without a husband fussing over politics and perhaps disturbing her rest. Carl saw the point, reluctantly, then left for America.

He reached Ohio in August, 1875; in spite of the heat, he plunged eagerly into the life he knew and liked best. With Agatha to help him, he traveled all over the state, concentrating on areas with large German populations.

His message obviously got through to the voters. Rutherford Hayes won by the slim margin of five thousand votes, with victory nailed down by a strong German turnout at the polls in Cincinnati.

For this Schurz received the grateful thanks of the party, and the friendship and respect of Hayes. He was urged to come back to the ranks of the regular Republicans, and let bygones be bygones.

It was a tempting offer and a flattering one, but Carl insisted on his independence. He would not commit himself until the Republicans nominated a presidential candidate.

So far, there were two possibilities—Grant himself, who let it be known that he would like a third term, and James G. Blaine, the Republican senator from Maine, a man of great influence but, according to Schurz, limited political vision.

Meantime, other matters pressed in on him. His newspaper badly needed his help. After Hayes' election, he returned to St. Louis and resumed his editorial duties, with Agatha acting as his housekeeper-secretary. "I sometimes feel," he told her after dinner one night, "that you're giving up all chances of happiness in order to take care of your father. Agatha, whatever happened to all the young men who used to come calling on you?"

She set a steaming cup of coffee before him. "They've been told to wait. There's room in my life for only one man at a time. And that man, right now, is you!"

Just before Christmas, he received a long letter from Margarethe saying she was feeling much stronger, and wasn't it time for her to be coming home, especially since she was expecting another baby in March? Carl immediately arranged for her return and was much relieved to find her in improved health, though her cough still persisted.

"It's this damp St. Louis weather," she said, making light of her illness.

"Then I'll sell my interest in the paper and we'll move out to California," he exclaimed. "I can just as well concern myself with politics under the sun as here."

"In the spring, Carl," she put him off. "After the baby comes."

Their child, another son, was born on March 5, 1876. Husband and wife were overjoyed and promptly named him Herbert, after Carl's late younger brother.

Happiness, however, was short-lived. A week later, Margarethe Schurz took a sudden turn for the worse and died peacefully in her sleep, her frail health no match for the exhausting strain of childbirth.

Carl was stunned by her loss. His wife had been close to him for nearly twenty-five years, a constant source of comfort in a tempestuous life. He could not imagine an existence without the calm and loyal Margarethe at his side. He felt limp; it was as if a hole had been ripped in his body and all the tremendous energy there had drained away.

"The loss of a wife of one's youth," he wrote to his friend, Dr. Abraham Jacobi, in New York, "is unlike any other bereavement. It is the loss of the best part of one's life." Then, knowing that Margarethe had spent her happiest years in Germany, he shipped her body there for burial in Hamburg.

Perhaps the greatest strain during this difficult time fell on Agatha's youthful shoulders. As the oldest of the four children—she was then twenty-three—Agatha pulled the demoralized family together, cared for the new baby and sent five-year-old Carl, Jr., toddling off to kindergarten. Marianne, of course, helped; together, the two girls did their best to help fill the void left by the untimely death of their mother.

The bereaved father remained inconsolable for months. He lost interest in his newspaper; he had no heart for politics. His mail piled up, opened by Agatha but unread by him. He sat in his shuttered, gloomy study day after day, impervious to the world outside. "The beauty of life is gone," he sighed to his daughter one evening. "I find it impossible to think about anything but your mother."

Agatha, wise beyond her years, fluffed a pillow behind his head. "Will you take the meerschaum tonight, Father." She held out his favorite pipe, determined to pull him out of self-pity. "Oh, I forgot to tell you, a package arrived today from Boston. A gift from Henry Cabot Lodge." She held up a jar of tobacco. "Just arrived from the Middle East, on one of the Lodge trading ships. And he expressly asked that you visit him—"

"Agatha!" Carl reached for his daughter's hand. "How much like your mother you look!"

"—next time you're in the East," she finished, refusing to feed his melancholy.

"And how much like her you sound, especially now, when you try to light a fire under this tired old carcass."

"Old, indeed!" She filled his pipe expertly. "And have you outstripped your usefulness at forty-eight?"

"Forty-seven, young lady!" He snatched the pipe from her. "Don't you try to push me beyond my years! Why, if I had a mind to—" He broke out into a sheepish grin. "I *have* been something of a trial these past few weeks, haven't I?" Then he snapped his fingers. "Which reminds me, we've got a lot of correspondence to clean up!" Carl lit the pipe and blew out a cloud of smoke. "Umm, this *is* good tobacco. Now, then, Agatha, do you suppose you can still take a letter?"

She was already at the desk, lighting the lamp. The family library hadn't been as cheerful since her mother . . . Agatha shook off her own memories. "I certainly can, unless you've forgotten how to dictate!"

Carl had not. Much to his relief, he found comfort in work, and a merciful release from painful recollections. Nor had he forgotten about his daughters and *their* future.

One evening, shortly after resuming his busy schedule, he called Agatha and Marianne to his study and reminded them that as far as he was concerned the period of mourning was over. "Time you two girls began entertaining young men again. Let's start with an informal tea this Sunday, yes? And

I promise not to play the piano. Unless I'm asked," he added with a grin.

His daughters agreed. Young men came to call on the Schurz girls. There were parties and dances in winter, picnics in summer. But after half a dozen visits it became clear to all that the two attractive daughters of former Senator Schurz had little time for prospective suitors. They were far too busy maintaining a household for their widowed father and his two growing boys.

11.

Once over his personal depression, Carl plunged back into politics. With another presidential campaign looming ahead, he found himself in a familiar dilemma: where to throw his support.

Backing an old-guard Republican like James Blaine was out of the question. It was equally hopeless to come out for Charles Adams, since the majority of the party would never support a liberal. For a while, Carl even considered another third-party move, despite the Greeley disaster four years before.

Happily, a compromise put an end to his problem. The Republicans chose Rutherford B. Hayes, the governor of Ohio, as their presidential hopeful, the very man Carl had helped put into the gubernatorial chair the year before!

The Democrats countered with Samuel Tilden, a quiet, philosophical lawyer of great distinction. Carl had no quarrel with Tilden, who was a noted liberal and an outspoken critic of Grant. Had the Republicans nominated anyone less moderate than Hayes, Carl might easily have jumped party lines that year.

But he had four good reasons for supporting the Ohio governor. First, Hayes was honest; second, he was an advocate of sound money; third, he was a moderate who would press for the completion of southern reconstruction; and fourth, as governor, Hayes had placed merit over patronage in filling state posts. "This could mean the real start of federal civil service reform," Schurz said hopefully. "But only if we get our man in the White House."

Carl stumped for Hayes from Boston to Mississippi and beyond. He held many private conversations with him, offering advice and help. When his key recommendations on such matters as civil service and sound money cropped up in Hayes' campaign promises, Schurz knew he had the candidate's ear.

However, he also argued with him. Once, for example, when Hayes "waved the bloody shirt"—a term used to remind voters that southern Democrats were rebels not too long ago and might be rebellious in the future—Schurz protested strongly. Hayes quickly changed his direction, fully aware of his adviser's influence among independent voters.

As election day approached, Hayes developed into a much more progressive candidate than he had been at the onset, thanks to men like Murat Halstead, Charles Adams and Carl Schurz. "I shall find many things to console me if defeated," Hayes told Carl at the end of the campaign, naming among them his close association with the former senator from Missouri.

Carl was singled out for another honor that year, one that added considerably to his reputation as a liberal leader. He was awarded an honorary degree of Doctor of Laws by Harvard University which, then as now, placed great emphasis on political leadership and freedom of thought.

The elections of 1876 brought about one of the classic controversies of American politics: should a presidential candidate who fails to win a majority of the popular vote move into the White House? Carl played a part in resolving this question—a small part, true, but as matters turned out, a significant one.

Election results that November had Tilden well ahead by

250,000 ballots, a comfortable enough margin considering the size of the total vote, some 8.4 million. The Democrats swept the key states of New York, New Jersey and Indiana, and claimed the entire South. The party's electoral count came to 203, eighteen more than was needed for victory. Carl Schurz went to bed that night convinced Tilden had won.

Next day, however, the picture changed dramatically. Three southern states, Louisiana, Florida and South Carolina, challenged the Democratic count in those states. They pointed to wholesale irregularities and fraud. Based on their own ballot count, they had Hayes out in front.

Carl made a quick check of the figures. If Republican claims were valid, then Rutherford Hayes would wind up the victor with 185 electoral votes, just enough to win the contest!

The Democrats refused to yield. The controversy between the two parties raged for days, during which time the United States had no President-elect, merely an outgoing Chief Executive. Confusion piled up as the three southern states (plus Oregon, which also contested election results) sent two groups to the electoral college, one representing each party. Carl Schurz shared the growing concern that unless some solution could be found quickly, the nation might be headed for disaster. Also, there were rumors that one or another candidate might seize the Presidency by force of arms.

"For anyone to win the highest office in the land in this manner would be a proceeding of doubtful character," Schurz warned both parties in January, 1877. Behind that understatement of the year was the clear intent of the idealist: play it fair!

He now joined a national movement to establish a bipartisan commission to settle the contested election. With the approval of Congress, which passed the Electoral Count Act of 1877, fifteen men were named to a commission: five senators, five representatives and five members of the Supreme Court. By agreement, the ten congressmen were equally divided between the two parties. Of the Supreme Court justices, two were Republicans, two Democrats; the four justices then joined in the unanimous choice of the fifth member.

Tilden accepted the plan without protest, but Hayes had second thoughts. The three southern states, after all, had legitimate protests. The Presidency should have been his, according to the constitutional powers granted the electoral college. Why send the decision to a commission? With the Army already behind Grant, it might take only a show of force to claim the election. Yet an adverse ruling could place the White House forever out of reach!

"That, Mr. Hayes, is the chance you'll have to take," Schurz bluntly told him. "I urge you, sir, not to dispute the commission but to accept its findings as the best—no, the only—solution now facing our democracy!"

Hayes, ever the realist, finally agreed. Weeks later, after long deliberation and much suspense, the commission announced its vote: for Tilden, seven; for Hayes, eight.

On March 5, 1877, Rutherford Birchard Hayes was duly sworn in as the nineteenth President of the United States, even though he had trailed in the popular vote by a quarter of a million ballots!

Historians have called Hayes' moderate administration the best thing that could have happened to a nation beset by economic difficulties and political intrigue. A practical man, he brought a sense of balance and reason to Washington where before there had been confusion and greed.

He also brought Carl Schurz back to the nation's capital

by naming him his Secretary of the Interior, the first United States citizen of German birth ever to hold a cabinet post.

Of the six others who then made up the cabinet, only one had any close association with the Grant administration. Hayes had promised to sweep Washington clean; he was now putting that promise into practice by bringing in men free of political taint. "He serves his party best," the new President proclaimed at his inaugural, "who serves his country best."

Hayes had made another campaign promise he was later to regret; if elected, he had said, he would serve for only one term, a self-imposed limitation intended to show the nation that he had no desire to build a political empire. This promise was to have a profound effect on Schurz's career.

But at the time, Carl was too excited over his appointment as Secretary of the Interior to think very much of the distant future. "We are all moving to Washington," he told his equally excited family in their St. Louis home. Carl, Jr., and Herbert, only children, nodded happily, but Agatha and Marianne were thrilled at the prospect of returning to the nation's capital.

Just about this time, Carl made an important decision. He was then only forty-nine, in the prime of life. He had thought several times of marrying again, more for the younger children's sake than his own. But when he saw that his two older daughters were happy with family life just as it was, he decided against taking another wife. Time to think about about that if either girl considered marriage for herself. Neither did. Each was content to fulfill her responsibilities in the Schurz household; Marianne cared for the children, while Agatha continued as her father's private secretary and housekeeper. It was an arrangement that was to last during Carl's long lifetime.

For their part, the two girls entered willingly into this family relationship. They knew their widowed father had no one else to turn to for help. His elderly mother, who might conceivably have taken care of the two boys, had died just before his appointment as Secretary, and his father had passed on in 1875. If ever a man needed a helping hand in holding together a family, it was Carl Schurz.

The Schurz family group descended on Washington in March, 1877. Carl rented a comfortable house not far from Capitol Hill and immersed himself in the complexities of his new job.

He soon learned that the post of Secretary of the Interior was a demanding one. "I am literally a jack of all trades," he told Agatha after his first day in the cabinet. "My job is a mixed bag of duties. It includes control over patents and pensions, over geological and geographical surveys, over public buildings here in Washington and national parks in every corner of the country. I'm also in charge of the Bureau of Indian Affairs, the Bureau of the Census and the Bureau of Education. In addition, my office looks after territories and the General Land Office."

Agatha smiled knowingly. "To say nothing of the Columbia Hospital for Women, the Asylum for the Deaf and the Dumb, and the Pagosa Hot Springs of Colorado. Here," she pushed a list toward her bewildered father, "I've already made a duty search of your office. It looks like nothing more than a dumping ground for government odds and ends."

It was just that. But within a month, his encyclopedic mind was in full command of a number of subjects ranging from Appalachian Mountain trails to zinc deposits in the expanding West.

His cabinet post gave the Secretary the long-awaited opportunity to put his civil service reforms into practice, if only in a limited way. He set up performance tests in the many federal bureaus under his authority. He weeded out incompetents and "dead wood," replacing them with qualified officeholders, regardless of their party affiliation. He punished those found guilty of corruption and bribery, and rewarded those with skill and devotion to duty.

President Hayes encouraged Carl by asking him to pass on these reforms to other departments in government. Soon the Schurz trademark began to crop up all over Washington. "Curse the fellow!" one old-time politician exclaimed. "He wants to run our department exactly as if it were a business!"

Resentment followed hard on the heels of reform. Some congressmen fought Schurz at every turn, especially in committees which controlled federal spending. Thus, commissions he appointed to study merit systems abroad were given hardly enough money for stationery and stamps. His own department was frequently short-changed. But the Secretary fought back. He was now finally beginning to understand that it was not enough merely to *believe* in reform; one must draw the sword and fight the enemy wherever he was found —in Congress, in committees or in the courts.

To Hayes' everlasting credit, he backed Schurz all the way. That year the slogan on Capitol Hill had a crusading ring: "Either conquer machine politics or surrender!"

The President did not surrender. In June, 1877, he issued an executive order that aimed at machine politicians. No federal employee, the order read, shall be required or permitted to take part in the management of political organizations, caucuses, conventions or election campaigns, or be forced to contribute to political fund drives. Shades of Ulysses S. Grant and his pressure tactics!

Secretary Schurz was delighted with the order. The fight

he had waged for so long, at such great odds, seemed to be bringing results at last. At the close of the Hayes administration, *Harper's Weekly* said of him: "We think Mr. Hayes has done more for the reform of civil service . . . than any President in our history."

To which Carl Schurz breathed a fervent "Amen!"

Perhaps nothing gave the new Secretary as much trouble in office as the situation he inherited in the Bureau of Indian Affairs.

The three previous administrations had left behind a tangle of laws, treaties and agencies in their efforts to deal with the problem of the red man. Since about 1850, the nation's inexorable drive to the West had systematically pushed Indians off their lands. The principal tribes affected were the Cheyenne, Sioux, Comanche, Arapaho and Pawnee. They saw their buffalo slaughtered by white invaders, their hunting grounds crisscrossed by railroads and telegraph lines; their tribal movements, once free, were now harassed by troops and white renegades.

By the time Schurz took over the Bureau in March, 1877, most of the plains Indians had been rounded up and placed on reservations in the vast area now known as Oklahoma, then called Indian Territory. It was the government's hope that once these tribes settled down, they would lead peaceful lives as farmers and sheepherders, thus allowing safe and orderly expansion of the West.

It turned out to be a forlorn hope. Few men in government were then aware of the near-impossible task of changing, in a relatively short time, the habits of a people who had lived for hundreds of years by hunting and fishing; yes, even raiding one another's villages. Nor could Washington do much about controlling the anger of many white settlers who felt the Indians were, literally, standing in the way of progress and profit. "The only good Indian," they freely admitted to one another, "is a dead Indian!"

The situation was further aggravated by a recent Indian uprising. Only months before Hayes' election, a band of aroused Sioux led by Chief Sitting Bull had annihilated an Army force led by Lieutenant Colonel George Custer at the Battle of the Little Big Horn, then fled over the Canadian border to escape United States authority. Other tribes in the Dakota and Montana wilderness proved equally troublesome, in part because the government did not always honor earlier agreements made with the Indians.

Feelings ran high on both sides. At times bands of vigilantes took matters in their own hands and raided Indian villages, some on protected reservations. The red men retaliated by massacring perfectly innocent white settlers. Army troops tried to keep order on the frontier with only partial success. Communications between Washington and Indian country frequently broke down. The American historian Carl Fuess, after examining many documents of that era, came to the conclusion that "our Indian policy, to put it mildly, had been short-sighted, unjust, and stupid."

And that was the policy Carl Schurz inherited as Secretary of the Interior!

He tried to put matters in order. He studied reports from Indian agents—government employees sent out to help tribesmen adjust to life on the reservation. He found some incompetent, some greedy and some downright arrogant. Supply contractors were worse; they not only cheated Indians out of supplies, but smuggled in rifles and cheap whiskey to them, both forbidden. And the military, Carl soon learned, was rigid and sometimes needlessly cruel in carrying out orders.

"Incredible!" he murmured as he began to get the whole picture of the Bureau. "Things can't be as bad as they look on paper. I must go see for myself!"

A six-week tour of Indian Territory convinced him that the situation was even worse. Taking his case to the President, he was told to "do what you can, Mr. Secretary, to tidy up the Bureau."

He received very little assistance from other branches of the government. Once, when he complained that the United States had deliberately broken an Indian treaty signed in 1865, he was told by Attorney-General Charles Devens that there was "no importance in a treaty made a dozen years ago with a pack of savages." Secretary of State William Evarts, an otherwise admirable lawyer, added that the pact in question was merely a gesture; that's all any treaties with Indians ever amounted to—gestures.

Carl was shocked. But in spite of public and private indifference, he began to clean house. First, he fired the Commissioner of Indian Affairs. When the replacement proved negligent, another was put in his place. Schurz also removed any agent convicted of graft or fraud. He trained new agents and enrolled Indians themselves for police operations, much to the horror of the military. Above all, he insisted that the Bureau remain in the Department of the Interior, and not be transferred to the War Department as the Army insisted. "Patience, not police action," was his motto. In time, he won that battle, too, which earned for him the grateful thanks of many Indian leaders.

He made another decision in line of duty which caught him in a crossfire from both sides—those who said he was being too lenient with the red man and those who said he was being too severe.

It all started when a band of three hundred Cheyenne—

men, women and children—decided Indian Territory was not for them. They wanted to go back to northern Wyoming from which they had originally come, even though it was a thousand miles away. The distance was nothing; being a nomadic tribe, they could easily travel on foot. Life on the reservation, they said, was impossible; the land was dry and dusty, they could not hunt; their squaws and children were sick with malaria, their braves seduced by firewater. The tribal chiefs told the Indian agent, an honest sort of fellow, that survival seemed more important just then than the law of the Great White Father in Washington.

They left the reservation in the dark of night in the hot summer of 1877. Next morning, the military commander at nearby Fort Reno sent out a company of soldiers to capture the Cheyenne, without a struggle if possible, and return them to the reservation. Those were his standing orders.

The soldiers found only bent grass, ashes of dead campfires, a broken arrow or two. It was as if the prairie had swallowed up the truant Indans.

A couple of days later, two lonely cowboys looking for a day's wages ran into the troops. They joined the hunt at a dollar a day. Later that week, they rode into a nearby town, filled themselves with whiskey and spread the rumor that the Army was hunting down a Cheyenne war party.

"Injuns!" Fear filled the countryside like a summer storm.

Armed vigilantes went out in pursuit. They were no more successful than the soldiers, for the Indians knew how to hide by day, travel by night. They also knew how to shoot their contraband rifles. A search party, stumbling on the fugitives' hiding place, was routed. Two whites were killed; the Cheyenne left three of their own dead behind.

"Injun war!" The scare jumped from white settlement to military post almost faster than the telegraph wires could carry the news. "Injun war!" There hadn't been an uprising in the plains country for years. Some bored settlers and drifters welcomed the promise of action. Frontier reporters, alert for developments, sent stories back to their newspapers, mixing fact and fancy in about equal proportions.

In Washington, Carl Schurz was besieged by inquiries. "Is there a war now going on between our troops and the Indians?" newspapermen asked him.

"There is no war, gentlemen," he assured them. "As far as I know, only a small band of Cheyenne are involved. Our military troops have been instructed to round them up, that's all. They are not to use force except in self-defense. It is a chase, nothing more."

The "chase" dragged on for weeks, then months. The Indians seemed to melt into endless prairie land; they knew how to forage and run and leave no trail behind. They crossed over into Kansas, with troops in vain pursuit.

When an isolated case of frontier murder or robbery occurred in the vicinity of the chase, the Cheyenne were blamed. Rumors built their number to twice, then three times the original number. Witnesses swore they saw Indian war parties swooping down on lonely settlements, burning and killing.

Reports of these atrocities filtered back to the Bureau of Indian Affairs. Carl Schurz studied them for hard evidence. He saw little to justify a massive counterattack as urged by some critics. As a matter of record, white settlers who were supposed to have been killed by the Cheyenne band showed up weeks later, hale and hearty. They had been on a cattle drive north, or out hunting in the hills. No, they had seen nothing of a war party, only a few Indians camping by a river, mostly women and children and a few old men.

Army units continued the hunt into Nebraska. The days

grew shorter, the weather colder. Once or twice, advance troops caught up with Cheyenne stragglers. Some gave up; some fought back. There were casualties on both sides. And still the Secretary of the Interior insisted this was no Indian war. Meantime, he was denounced by those who wanted to declare open warfare on the Cheyenne, as well as by those who wanted to call off the "wicked manhunt" as they called it.

Schurz held his ground, waiting for proof.

It came, finally, in November, 1878. A report told Carl all he wanted to know. It was addressed to him by the military commander at Fort Robinson, Nebraska, some seven hundred miles northwest of Indian Territory. What he read in that detailed document made him bow his head in horror, anger and shame.

About half the escaping Cheyenne had been captured, the report began, mostly women, children, a dozen braves and an old chief—maybe a hundred in all. The rest of the tribe had gotten away, probably heading for the Wyoming hills, Cheyenne country. The report explained that the hundred-odd captives had been placed under guard at the fort, in a long shack, a sort of blockhouse. They had been told that they would be kept there until they promised to return peacefully to their reservation in Indian Territory. If they agreed, the Army would take them back in wagons and feed them on the way. No one would be arrested, the report went on to say, except those who planned the escape.

The Indians had refused. The Cheyenne chief told the fort commander that the tribe would rather die than go back to Indian Territory.

In an effort to break their will, the commander decided to deny them food and water. Perhaps, the report suggested, if the women and children suffered a little, the men would change their minds.

They had not. The whole group, as a matter of fact, had made a break for it that very night. Two sentries had been killed, even though the Indians had been searched for weapons, according to regulations. The report was explicit: the soldiers did not fire until fired upon first; a case of self-defense, all the way. The troopers, of course, had given chase. All through that bitter cold night and through three more days and nights, they had tracked down the escaped fugitives. It was unavoidable, but many of the Indians had died in the break from the blockhouse—some from exposure, some by drowning in the nearby half-frozen White River, many by bullets. Included among the casualties were a number of women and children. An unfortunate incident certainly, the report concluded. But the Army after all, was acting under orders from Washington.

Carl Schurz rubbed his eyes wearily, then turned to a huge map of the plains country. He measured the distance from Indian Territory to the Wyoming hills, where the survivors were said to be heading. How many were left out of the original three hundred, the Secretary wondered. A hundred? Perhaps.

"A thousand miles on foot through the wilderness," he muttered half-aloud. "And all in search of freedom!"

Then, measuring law against human need, troops against Indians, compassion against penalty, Carl Schurz made his decision.

Later that winter, a United States Army search patrol finally caught up with the rest of the fugitive Cheyenne tribe. They caught up with them because the Indians were no longer running; they had come home at last, in the mountains and valleys of Wyoming and Montana. And they did not hide because they were too tired and sick; also because the Army officer was advancing under a flag of truce.

"The Great White Father in Washington," the officer told the old chief who had made it back to the hills, "has given permission for you to remain here on your former hunting grounds. You will never have to return to Indian Territory. You and your people may live here for a thousand moons." Then he turned away, sickened at the wretched condition of those who had somehow survived the ordeal.

Schurz soon realized that the American Indian's greatest need was the freedom to learn, to acquire new skills so that he could take part in the social and economic life of the nation. As a pilot project, he enrolled fifty Indian boys in Virginia's Hampton Institute, a trade and agricultural school organized just after the Civil War for young Negroes.

"It'll never work," his critics scoffed. "You just can't tame those red savages!"

The experiment worked magnificently. Dozens of Indian graduates of Hampton were sent back to their reservations each year with skills never before made available to the red man—carpentry, scientific farming, animal husbandry, printing and metal forging.

Schurz also helped organize the famous Carlisle Indian School in Pennsylvania during his term of office. He pleaded with Congress for funds, then worked tirelessly to find dedicated teachers so that promising young Indians could get an education in all subjects, including liberal arts and the professions. The Carlisle School flourished until the end of World War I when it closed its doors only because American Indians could then enroll almost anywhere without restriction.

Carl Schurz's work with the Indians turned one of his severest critics into an admirer. Thomas Nast, who once caricatured Schurz as the devil himself, now drew noble sketches of him as the Secretary of the Interior cleaning out the Bureau of Indian Affairs and ridding it of its baleful gnomes of "corruption, apathy and ignorance."

To Schurz's impressive record was added one more achievement: he was one of the nation's earliest conservationists. As Secretary of the Interior, he asked for legislation to halt the shameful waste of the nation's fields and forests, to set aside virgin park lands, to control the sale of timberland and to make it mandatory for one small tree to be planted where a large one was cut down.

He found few supporters. His old political enemy, Senator Blaine, attacked his proposals as "imported Prussian methods" which had no place in the United States. Carl, indeed, had taken the trouble to study forest preservation in Germany, where hundreds of thousands of timberland acres had been saved in a country so much smaller than his own. He was also attacked by lumber barons in Wisconsin and Minnesota who resented "federal intervention in the affairs of sovereign states."

Meantime, the reckless cutting down of trees went on. In the end, the states with their depleted forests were the losers. Not until a quarter of a century later, when Theodore Roosevelt made conservation a national issue, did America recognize the need to preserve her natural resources. Happily, Carl was still alive then, and very much tempted to say, "I told you so!"

In spite of these and other problems, Schurz very much wanted to stay on as Secretary of the Interior, but President

Hayes refused to run for re-election. "I said four years ago that I would not run again," he reminded Schurz who asked him to reconsider, "and I will not."

When Hayes stepped down in 1880, the people chose another Republican, James Garfield, to succeed him. Schurz supported him as a moderate candidate and even took the stump for him, though he knew very well that Garfield had the privilege of bringing in his own cabinet members, which he did, by naming Samuel Jordan Kirkwood as the incoming Secretary of the Interior. But if Schurz moved out of the cabinet, his influence did not. Kirkwood subsequently carried out most of his predecessor's Indian program without change.

Before leaving Washington, Carl sent an informal report to President-elect Garfield. "I shall never forget the trials I had to go through during the first period of my administration," he wrote, "and the mistakes that were made before I had things well in hand. It is a constant fight with the sharks that surround the Indian Bureau, the Pension Office, and the Patent Office, and a ceaseless struggle with perplexing questions and situations, especially in the Indian Service."

Then, with a mischievous sense of humor, he concluded his message to Garfield thus: "I congratulate you and the country most sincerely on your election . . . your real troubles will now begin!"

12.

Carl was in rare good humor for a man about to lose a well-paying job in a city he enjoyed. He had his reasons for optimism.

Just after Garfield's victory, he had been offered the job as associate editor on the New York *Evening Post,* a liberal daily. Carl accepted eagerly, even though it meant sharing duties with Edwin Godkin, a brilliant writer but difficult to get along with; he had met him several times before, both in and out of government.

Carl was happy about being back in New York, and his tall figure, with its jaunty stride, fitted handsomely with the city's vibrant existence. Furthermore, he hoped the change of scene might induce his two daughters to expand their social contacts. This they did, but only as they related to the Schurz household. Agatha and Marianne became the hostesses for dinner parties given by their father for his newspaper friends and associates. They frequently were seen at the theater with him, more often Agatha than Marianne, who continued looking after the two younger boys. Carl recognized his daughters' devotion with a certain poignancy. More than once he reminded them that they had lives of their own to lead. But they brushed aside his paternal concern and continued to run the family without complaint or conflict. They were a source of great comfort to him, especially since they went about their various duties cheerfully and without a hint of self-pity.

He especially enjoyed renewing his friendship with Dr. Abraham Jacobi, now a prominent physician in New York. The doctor was of great help to Schurz in the move from city to city. He found him a fine apartment close to Central Park, suggested a suitable school for the two Schurz boys and introduced Carl to many of the civic-minded citizens of the community. The friendship between these two former German refugees deepened over the years. Each, in turn, became a source of comfort to the other.

Schurz kept a close editorial eye on Garfield during the President's first few months in office. He had supported Garfield, but not with a great deal of enthusiasm; he was now prepared to renew that support or attack him, depending on his moves, especially in civil service affairs.

The President barely had a chance to prove himself. Less than five months after taking office, an assassin's bullet cut him down. Hovering painfully between life and death for many weeks, Garfield finally died on September 19, 1881, the innocent victim of a disgruntled office seeker.

The tragedy shocked the nation. Editor Schurz called the killing a double tragedy. "Not only have we lost a competent President," he wrote, "but a man who promised much in the way of government reform. The fight for the merit system must continue."

Privately, he felt less confident. Garfield's successor, former Vice President Chester A. Arthur, was a member of the Republican old guard. Schurz now supposed that much of his previous work in civil service would be swept away. He was therefore doubly thankful that the year before he had helped organize the National Civil Service League, a private group which kept a close watch over government hiring practices and advised on federal job appointments.

Carl and the League were both pleasantly surprised when

President Arthur, in one of those strange turnabouts, came out in favor of the merit system. On second thought, Carl decided, perhaps it wasn't so strange. The Civil Service League had developed into an influential group, with a number of strong chapters in the East. Its leaders were well known: George Williams Curtis, the editor; Henry Adams, the historian; Henry Cabot Lodge, then a young member of the Massachusetts state legislature; Theodore Roosevelt, the future "Rough Rider"; and of course, Carl Schurz who was on intimate terms with all of them.

President Arthur could hardly ignore such distinguished company. He therefore asked Congress for a law that would give official status to the merit system. The result was the highly successful Pendleton Act, drawn up by Senator George Pendleton, Democrat of Ohio, and signed by President Arthur in 1883. This is still the basis of today's federal civil service system.

In essence, the Pendleton Act had three important provisions: a three-man commission appointed by the President; second, a graded classification system for clerks in all federal bureaus; and third, competitive examinations for all clerical, professional and trade service jobs in the government. It was a notable victory for Carl Schurz, who had struggled for so long against the spoils system, and since the measure was nearly identical with the bill he himself had introduced in the Senate fifteen years before.

He also derived much satisfaction from his newspaper job. He was happy to be back in the profession and to be surrounded by prominent colleagues in business, politics and the professions. More and more, they sought him out to ask his advice on the affairs of the day. He was fast becoming an "elder statesman" among independents, in spite of the fact that he had yet to reach his fifty-fourth birthday in 1883.

Carl's advisory role pleased him enormously. The liberal wing of the Republican party seldom took a step without consulting him, while conservatives thought twice before pushing a bill that might incur the personal and editorial wrath of this political eagle whose influence seemed to have increased rather than decreased since his Washington days.

There was, however, one annoying problem. Schurz could not get along with Edwin Godkin, the associate editor of the *Post*. Both were strong-minded men, both reformers, both had a vision of ideal government. Godkin was an aristocrat, believing that only the wealthy and educated should lead society. Carl, of course, could agree to no such philosophy.

Had their arguments been limited to philosophical questions, the two might never have come to a parting of the ways. But they locked horns editorially over a prominent labor issue. When railway telegraphers went on strike in the summer of 1883, Godkin denounced them with all the arrogance of his aristocratic station, while Carl defended them with all the passion of his "common man" background.

The *Post* fairly sizzled with their conflicting views. The resulting clash of personalities in the editorial room often drowned out the jangle of the paper's presses.

In this intolerable situation Carl offered his resignation, perhaps with the hope that the publisher might support *his* point of view. To his dismay, the publisher did not, and Schurz had no choice but to go through with his decision.

It could not have happened at a worse time. Carl's financial status, never very strong, now collapsed due to some poor investments he had made. He still held part ownership of the St. Louis *Westliche Post,* but this brought little return, barely enough to pay for the rental of his New York apartment. With four children to support—Carl, Jr., and Herbert were both in school—he was forced to exercise the most stringent economies.

Word of his financial plight soon reached sympathetic ears. A group of affluent German-Americans started a fund of $100,000 to be presented to him as a living memorial. Their sincere thinking was that the man who had done so much for others should now have something done for him.

Carl heard of the plan and quickly killed it. "I am touched by your esteem," Schurz told financier Gustav Schwab when the latter called on him. "But I cannot accept a penny without an equivalent return. Since there is no prospect of doing so in the immediate future, I must reluctantly refuse your most generous offer."

Schwab answered with far less formality. "In heaven's name, Carl, look at it as an outright gift . . . with no strings attached!"

"No strings for you, my dear Schwab. But I would be forever under the obligation of your committee if I were to accept the money which, goodness knows, I need. But I need my independence more." He smiled wryly. "What would happen, for example, if in some future political matter I did not agree with you or the German-American community? You would have every right to say to me, 'Carl, we need your support. Remember the one hundred thousand?' And I would have to remember, Gus. A poor man like me does not forget a large sum so easily."

"Fair enough," Schwab agreed. "I respect your independence, but deplore your nose for financial affairs. However are you going to get by?"

"Something will turn up," he assured his guest. "Something always does to keep this poor dog in bone."

True to his prediction, help arrived in the next week's mail. While still with the *Post,* Schurz had discussed the possibility of writing a biography of Henry Clay and had submitted a chapter and a detailed outline. In the mail that very morning was a contract from the publisher, and an advance of one thousand dollars!

Carl waved the check in boyish delight. "Manna from heaven!"

Agatha snatched it from his fingers. "You're so right, Father. The baker, the butcher and the man from the gas company have been in the kitchen for a week, drinking my coffee and waiting for payment. Here, sign this check so I can send them away!"

"Did you say coffee?" He grinned, patting his stomach. "I really do have an appetite this morning. I believe I'll have hot cereal, eggs, sausage, a bit of strudel—"

"You'll have coffee and a poached egg and that's all! Or did you forget, Father, you never work well on a full stomach?" Behind Agatha's firmness was a warm respect for the man she admired more than any other. She sat him at his desk, running her eyes over the contract. "Seems in order, though we'd better revise the length of the manuscript. With the material we've been gathering on Clay, there's enough in our files for *two* volumes!"

She was right. When finally published in 1887, the biography of Henry Clay by Carl Schurz ran to two volumes of four hundred pages each. It was hailed everywhere as the finest account to date of the "Great Compromiser," the self-educated Kentuckian who had saved the Union three times with his compassionate legislation.

Carl was immensely pleased with the book's reception. It had taken him four years to write it, not too long when one considers the monumental character of the biography.

It might have been finished sooner had Carl not heeded another call to the political wars in the summer of 1884. But had he not, the course of American history might have been irrevocably changed.

The call came a year after Carl began work on the Clay book. He had, in the meantime, read all of Clay's congressional debates; he had examined his private papers, visited many of the towns and villages where Clay had lived, interviewed all survivors who remembered him, in short, had been busy with basic research, always the sign of a good scholar.

Carl was working in the study of his New York apartment in the late spring of 1884, dictating to Agatha, when the cry of a newsboy's "Wuxtra!" drifted through the open window. In those days without radio and television, news bulletins were first announced by hordes of newsboys who took to the streets with stacks of special editions, called "extras," and hawked them to eager readers.

"Wuxtra! Wuxtra!" The garbled cries rang through the streets. Annoyed at the interruption, Agatha got up to close the window.

"No, leave it open!" Carl laid down a sheaf of notes. "I thought I heard—listen!"

Father and daughter froze in silence.

"Wuxtra!" they heard the chant. "Blaine gets it! Read all about it! Wuxtra!"

"Blaine!" Carl rushed to the window. "Boy, here!" He tossed a coin to the sidewalk. "Agatha, run downstairs—! Never mind, I'll do it myself!" He dashed out, his dressing robe trailing behind him.

Agatha returned to her father's desk, collecting his scattered notes. She, too, understood the cry of "Wuxtra! Blaine gets it!" The Republican National Convention, meeting in Chicago that week, had apparently nominated James Blaine for the Presidency of the United States.

She repeated the name, half-aloud, then shook her head. Her father's lifelong political enemy! Agatha Schurz knew only too well that he would never return to his book until he had done his utmost to keep Blaine from reaching the White House.

To understand something of Carl's violent reaction, it is necessary to know more of James Blaine.

He had been an important newspaper editor in Maine, long-time chairman of the state Republican party and congressman from that state from 1863 to 1876. He had also been Speaker of the House of Representatives during the years Schurz had served in the Senate. A party politician to his immaculate fingertips, Blaine had tried once before to get the presidential nomination, only to be blocked by Rutherford Hayes, aided and abetted by Schurz himself. He had never forgiven Carl for that defeat. Later, as a senator from Maine during Schurz's term as Secretary of the Interior, he had taken a measure of revenge by defeating the Secretary's forest conservation program and by sniping at his recommendations for civil service and Indian affairs.

The enmity between these two contrasting figures was deep-rooted. Schurz was a liberal Republican, often crossing party lines. Blaine, on the other hand, was known as a "half-breed" Republican, only slightly less conservative than Conkling and Morton, but still a leader in the old guard. On any important issue, chances were good that Blaine would be on one side, Schurz on the other.

But it was Blaine's complicity in the famous "Mulligan letters" that really set Carl against him.

The Mulligan letters had first come to light in 1875. A congressional investigating committee, led by Democrats, had charged Blaine with corrupt practices during the time he served as Speaker of the House. The committee was specific; it offered evidence that Blaine had used his influence to secure a favorable land grant for the Little Rock Railroad Company in Arkansas, then sold the company's bonds at a liberal commission, thus amassing a private fortune for himself.

"Prove it!" Blaine challenged his accusers.

The committee cited the Mulligan letters, a series of incriminating notes which Blaine had written a railroad official of that name, hinting that he, as Speaker of the House, could be of considerable help to the company. "I do not feel that I shall be a dead-head in this enterprise," he wrote in one letter. Another ended with the phrase: "Burn this letter!" The committee said that it would present the evidence at the proper time.

When the "proper time" came, the Mulligan letters could not be found. The wily Blaine had taken the opportunity to secure the correspondence through devious means.

The evidence in question suddenly appeared a week later, but this time in the possession of Blaine himself. He then proceeded to make dramatic use of his letters to Mulligan, reading them aloud before the rapt attention of the House of Representatives. But he selected only favorable portions, and even these he read out of chronological order. The total effect was to give the impression of a man wronged in the service of his country.

Blaine's defense crumbled years later when the full texts of the Mulligan letters were published. At the time of the investigation, however, he escaped censure from the committee. But not from Carl Schurz. "That man," he was heard to mutter after the case was closed, "is corruption personified. I will continue to fight him anytime, anywhere, in any political arena in the land!"

That arena was set larger than life in the presidential campaign of 1884. On the Republican side was the suave, affluent, often brilliant James Blaine. On the Democratic side was the stolid, ponderous Grover Cleveland, the industrious governor of New York State. Carl Schurz now thrust himself into the impending battle on the side of the Democrats, announcing his position in an uncompromising letter to former President Rutherford Hayes, with whom he still maintained a close friendship.

"I oppose Blaine," Carl Schurz wrote on July 27, 1884, "because I believe that the election to the Presidency of the United States of a man who wrote the Mulligan letters, and who stands before the country as the representative of the practices they disclose, would be a precedent fraught with incalculable evil—a fatal blow to the moral foundations of our republican government. It would be a terrible thing to teach our young people that such a record does not disqualify a man for the highest honors and trusts of the Republic. . . . I solemnly declare my belief that . . . nothing a Democratic administration may bring with it can possibly be as bad . . . as the mere fact of Mr. Blaine's election!"

Never one to let words alone stand, Schurz took immediate action. He sounded out key Republican leaders; did they share his feelings about Blaine?

Many did, much to Carl's relief. He met with such notables as President Charles Eliot of Harvard, the Reverend Henry Ward Beecher, editor George Putnam, Moorefield Storey, the Boston lawyer who was later to become the first President of the National Association for the Advancement of Colored People, and Ralph Waldo Emerson, the writer and philosopher. All agreed they could not support a man like Blaine.

During an early meeting with anti-Blaine Republicans, someone made an offhand remark about Grover Cleveland. "We love him," an unknown gentleman said, "for the enemies he has made."

That phrase became their watchword. In a matter of days they were also to have a name. The New York *Tribune* labeled the independent group "Mugwumps," not altogether a flattering term. The name itself was of Indian origin, meaning "head man" or "chief." Perhaps the *Tribune* felt that the Schurz-led Republicans had cornered the market on party leaders in their war against Blaine. If so, the paper was only partly right. Many prominent Republicans stayed with the party, more than went over to the independents. But Mugwumps they were and Mugwumps they remained all through the hectic campaign of 1884.

Carl Schurz fairly gloried in that label. "People won't soon forget it," he enthused, "or what it stands for, provided we work hard to keep that name alive."

The work he spoke of began in earnest when the Mugwumps called a national conference which met in New York in July, 1884. Carl was one of its most tireless leaders. He was appointed chairman of its Committee on Resolutions. Later, he was put in charge of the national committee that ran the independents' campaign, raising money, publishing pamphlets and sending out speakers in behalf of Grover Cleveland. No one that summer and fall spoke with as much dedication of purpose as Schurz, or as often.

The Mugwump movement was unique in American politics. Nothing like its size and influence had been seen before among independent Republicans. One of Schurz's key jobs as a Mugwump was to swing important Republicans over to Cleveland. In this he succeeded frequently; he also had his failures, particularly in the person of Henry Cabot Lodge. Carl carried on a long and cordial correspondence with the young lawyer from Massachusetts, who was then running for the House of Representatives. "Be reasonable, Cabot," he urged. "Blaine will only trample on your ideals. Come over to our side while there is still time."

"I am being reasonable, if nothing else," Lodge replied. "By staying in the party I can be of some use to the Republicans. By going out I destroy all influence and power for good I possess." Lodge lost his election to Congress that year but never left the party which he later served as senator for nearly forty years.

Perhaps no single event in the 1884 campaign equaled the scandal that almost deflated the Cleveland boom. Mugwumps and Democrats alike were dismayed when the shocking story broke that Grover Cleveland, ten years before, had had an affair with a woman who had born him a son out of wedlock.

Stunned Mugwumps met over dinner that night, their gloom as thick as the cigar smoke swirling over coffee and brandy. "All is lost!" one of them sighed.

"We haven't a chance," another agreed.

"Blaine now has the field all to himself," a third mourned.

So it went around the melancholy table until the turn passed to Schurz. Carl kept his silence until everyone looked up. Then he lit a fresh cigar.

"Have we forgotten something, gentlemen?" His eyes glared through the smoke like a pair of searchlights. "The issue here is not our candidate's private life! The issue is honesty in government! However blameless Blaine may be in his personal dealings, his public life and record are the real target! That's our job, to make voters see the men as presidential candidates, not husbands!"

Cleveland never denied the scandal. He admitted his past indiscretions, then continued to press his party's platform—low tariffs, sound money and extension of constitutional rights for all citizens.

Schurz's zeal in behalf of the Mugwumps never lagged. In one twelve-day period, he spoke in Detroit, then swung down to Ohio where he addressed crowds in Toledo, Cleveland,

Mansfield, Dayton, Cincinnati, Portsmouth, Columbus, Wooster and Canton—the well-traveled campaigner, in every sense of the word. At every stop he hammered away at the Mulligan letters, Blaine's Achilles' heel!

One of the most important—and least expected—assists for the Democrats came from a Blaine supporter, a New York clergyman named Samuel Burchard. As a spokesman for his fellow clerics, he promised to help Blaine in every way, then added: "We are Republicans, and don't propose to leave our party and identify ourselves with the party whose antecedents have been *Rum, Romanism, and Rebellion.*" In trying to repudiate the Mugwumps, the unfortunate clergyman had raised the triple specter of prohibition, anti-Catholicism, and the "bloody shirt"!

The statement created a sensation. All sorts of explanations were issued about what the Reverend Burchard *meant* to say in behalf of the Republicans. But it was too late; the damage had been done.

The election was close. Grover Cleveland edged out James Blaine by an electoral count of 219 to 182. The winning margin was supplied by New York State which went Democratic by the slim plurality of 1,149 votes.

Many factors contributed to Cleveland's victory. His candor in admitting past mistakes was one. So were the cartoons of Thomas Nast, who long ago had switched to Schurz's side. The *Rum, Romanism, and Rebellion* speech also helped.

But it was the Mugwumps that kept Cleveland in the running and made it possible for him to overtake Blaine. By building up solid support for the Democratic candidate among Republican ranks, they were able to switch enough votes to put Cleveland in the White House, the first Democrat in that post since Buchanan.

Schurz's leadership role among the Mugwumps was undeniable. According to historian Fuess, "He was the engine which drove the machinery along. Without him the movement could not have gathered momentum as rapidly as it did."

Thus, to the many honors and titles already to his credit, the friends of Carl Schurz added another: President-maker.

Once Blaine had been defeated, Carl slowed down his feverish pace. Now past fifty-five, he took greater advantage of the rich cultural life of New York. He attended more operas and concerts, and went to the theater frequently. He met Mark Twain; the two gentlemen from Missouri struck up an immediate friendship that lasted for many years. He also played the piano more regularly. Never very shy about any of his talents, Carl delighted himself and his friends by giving informal concerts at home. A typical social evening at the Schurzes, with Agatha and Marianne as hostesses, included port, politics, a piano concert and more politics.

He also spent a great deal of time with his sons, Carl, Jr., then thirteen, and Herbert, eight. The devoted father took many long walks with them through Central Park and was never too busy to discuss their schoolwork. His personal knowledge of historical figures made his sons' eyes fairly pop. "You mean you *knew* Lincoln?" Herbert once asked him.

"Knew him, son? Why many's the time I sat as close to him as I am now to you. We were talking about the time. . . ." And off he launched on some story of the election campaign. Or he talked of Stephen Douglas, or the Civil War, or his differences with Ulysses Grant. In time, the boys made their father a willing victim of a harmless game. Whenever homework weighed too heavily on them, they innocently asked if their father had ever met Salmon Chase or Hamilton Fish or some other figure of the recent past. Whereupon the delighted parent would regale his sons with firsthand accounts that made history come to glowing life.

As always, there was the necessity of providing for his family. Carl picked up where he had left off last June on the biography of Henry Clay. When the publisher's advance ran out, he went on an extensive lecture tour in the winter of 1884–85. Then it was back to Clay for another year of writing, interrupted by frequent speaking engagements, debates and the writing of articles, all of which added to his meager bank account.

There's no telling how long it would have taken to complete the Clay biography had it not been for an unfortunate accident early in 1887—unfortunate for Carl, that is, and most fortunate for the publisher. Returning home one cold, blustery night in February, Schurz slipped on a patch of ice and broke his leg.

He was approaching sixty then but still in vigorous health. "Any other man his age would have spent six months in bed with that fractured thigh," said Dr. Jacobi later. "But I had all I could do to keep him quiet for ten weeks."

The mending of that broken leg kept Carl on his back, forcing him to concentrate on the Clay manuscript. He finished it that spring, much to the relief of his publisher. That fall, after the book was published and well received, Carl called his family together.

"Your father," he began solemnly, trying to hide the twinkle in his eye, "is seriously thinking of embarking on another career."

Agatha groaned, knowing any new venture would put more burdens on her already overworked shoulders. Carl pretended not to hear her sounds of distress.

"Oh, yes," he went on. "I was thinking I might give my full time over to writing. As a matter of fact, I'm thinking of starting another life story."

Agatha was visibly relieved, while the two boys let out shouts of delight. "Who will it be this time, Father?" young Carl asked. "General Grant?"

"Oh, someone I know much better!"

"Abraham Lincoln, then!" Herbert guessed.

"Better known to me than even Old Abe!"

Herbert wanted to know if it was George Washington.

"Washington? Look here, young man, how old do you think I am, anyway?"

Marianne, who had caught the spirit of the game, clapped her hands. "All right, we give up. Whose biography are you going to do of the man you know better than Grant or Lincoln?"

Carl kept a straight face with effort. "I thought—that is, if anyone here showed any interest in it, I might do the life and times of . . . of Carl Schurz! Yes, and don't look so startled, my fine young friends! When a man approaches sixty, he looks backward, not forward!"

Agatha put a hand on his shoulder, a hint of tears in her eyes. "I think that would be a wonderful book, Father. Of course we think you should write it, and I'll do all I can to help. When do we start?"

"Next spring, when school lets out for the boys."

"Can we help, too?" they asked in unison.

"No, but I thought you might like to come along while I refreshed my memories of old friends and places. Tell you what, children, how would you all like to spend a year with me, in Germany?"

They all sailed for Europe in June, 1888, and spent a happy

ten months traveling about the Rhine Valley, Rostatt, Munich, Berlin, Zurich and London, all the places Schurz had been in his tempestuous youth. Agatha's eyes grew wide as she learned more of her father's past. "A revolutionary! Really, Father, what would your political friends at home say if they knew?"

"I mean for them to know, Agatha. Maybe it'll show them how a reformer is put together and what makes him tick. Come, today we visit the prison at Spandau from where I helped Dr. Kinkel escape when he was held prisoner by the king of Prussia."

Herbert's mouth fell open. "Will they arrest you for that now?"

Carl suppressed a smile. "That, my boy, is a chance I'll have to take."

He was, of course, only teasing. No one need have any fears about his return to Spandau. Nearly forty years had passed since that daring prison break. None of the principals were now alive except for Carl and one of the Donath twins, Emil, who still drove a carriage in the suburbs of Berlin. Waldemar Brume, the guard, was gone; Kinkel was dead; only Spandau remained, as bleak and forbidding as ever.

After his leisurely journey into the past, Carl was given a farewell dinner by his old friends in Bonn. "My fatherland," he told them, "still holds many attractions for me, and I am tempted to live out my years here, among dear friends and precious memories. But there is a greater pull from across the ocean, where all my children were born, and where so much work yet remains to be done. I return, therefore, with fond remembrances of the past, but with fonder hopes for the future."

13. A changed political scene greeted Carl on his return to the United States in the winter of 1888. Benjamin Harrison, a traditional Republican, had defeated Grover Cleveland for the Presidency, the first national election since 1856 in which Schurz had not played a significant part. Some of his friends wondered if his political ardor had cooled.

They had good reason for thinking so. While in Europe, Schurz had agreed to manage the New York office of the Hamburg-American Steamship Company, a job which now took up all his time. He spent long hours over figures and accounts; the work was dull but the salary was good. For the next three years he remained politically inactive, content to trade personal involvement for financial security.

But when maneuvering for another presidential election began late in 1891, the reformer-turned-businessman found it difficult to remain behind his desk. For one thing, he had had his fill of the conservative Harrison. For another, he was bored with business routine. When Grover Cleveland let it be known that he would be willing to make another run at Harrison, Carl resigned his job and plunged once more into the political world he knew so well.

His decision was made easier by an offer from *Harper's Weekly,* whose editor, George William Curtis, was ailing and needed help. Carl was hired as an assistant editorial writer;

his first task was to send out a call to liberals and former Mugwumps. Would they work for Harrison's defeat and Cleveland's nomination?

They responded with an emphatic "Yes!" But New York City's Tammany machine wasn't so sure. It tried to ring in its own man at the Democratic convention, which made Schurz, an implacable foe of the Tiger, work all the harder. It was no contest as Cleveland won the nomination on the first ballot.

Carl's voice in behalf of the liberals grew even stronger when he became chief editorial writer for *Harper's* after Curtis died in the summer of 1892. The promotion also had its financial rewards for which Carl was thankful. Carl, Jr., was already in college, while Herbert had set his sights on Harvard.

The campaign that year was free of mud-slinging, which gave Schurz an excellent opportunity to display his editorial skills. Writing in his publication, he made this incisive comment about Cleveland: "He has a conscience. He has a will. He has a patriotic heart. He has a clear head. He has a strong sense of right. He has a good knowledge of affairs. He is a party man but not a party slave. He is true to duty regardless of personal interest."

Few candidates have ever had a testimonial as direct and simple. But in those days of editorial hyperbole, few men wrote with the logic and economy of Carl Schurz.

Cleveland was elected by a comfortable margin in 1892. Carl, too, enjoyed a triumph of sorts that year when he was named head of the National Civil Service League, succeeding the recently deceased Curtis.

It was in this post that Carl came to know better another towering figure in American history, Theodore Roosevelt. Not everything had gone smoothly between the two men up until then; nor were they to agree on other issues later on. Roosevelt had had nothing but disdain for Schurz in his role as Mugwump leader, while Carl had opposed young Teddy when the latter ran for mayor of New York City in 1886. But when it came to civil service, the veteran Schurz and the youthful Roosevelt worked hand in hand for a cause in which they both believed passionately. Together they nearly drove the newly elected President to distraction. "Some of my friends," Cleveland complained good-naturedly, "seem to think that the government is to be conducted merely for the purpose of civil service reform."

The next few years passed happily for Carl Schurz and his family. Herbert entered Harvard in 1893; Carl, Jr., now a lawyer, married the year after. With his household reduced by two, the elder Schurz and his two daughters took a home in Pocantico Hills, a rural retreat some twenty-five miles north of New York City. He also kept an apartment in the city which he and Agatha occupied during the winter months. Altogether, he led a pleasant, active life, enjoying the best of town and country.

Carl no longer troubled his mind about his daughters' future. Both had passed what was then considered "the marriageable age." But far from resenting their single state, both women did their best to make life pleasant for themselves and their elderly parent. Agatha went with him to lectures and concerts, and frequently read to him when his eyes tired. Marianne continued to look after the boys whenever they visited at home.

It was just about this time that his close friend and companion, Dr. Abraham Jacobi, took him to Lake George, where the doctor maintained a summer cottage on the cool, pine-covered shores of the lake, some two hundred miles north of the city. Here he spent many happy hours, tramping through the woods, fishing or just sitting on the porch.

Meantime, he continued to write for *Harper's,* commenting on a wide variety of subjects. He also worked on his autobiography, portions of which later appeared in *McClure's,* one of the more popular magazines of his day. Aside from revealing Schurz as a writer of great charm—he described his early boyhood in these chapters—they furnished him with the necessary income to send his son to college and maintain two modest households.

When a man begins to make his private life public, it is generally thought he is ready for retirement. No one, so his friends told him, had earned that right more than he. But they did not take into account Carl's deep moral involvement in the issues of the day.

England in the 1890's was a great power, supreme on land and sea. Germany, after finally having been unified under Bismarck, was under the command of King William II, the modern Kaiser with strong ambitions for colonial conquest. He therefore built up a strong army and navy. A wary France followed suit. And Spain, once a mighty military force, was struggling to keep her far-flung empire intact.

Only the United States seemed behind the times, militarily. Many well-meaning citizens now began to raise a clamor for America's "place in the sun." They advocated military preparedness in order to keep pace with England, Germany and France. The more bellicose champions of military strength—and Theodore Roosevelt was one of them, much to Schurz's disgust—were called "jingoes" or "jingoists." The aging editor of *Harper's* took a long look at the gathering forces of war and promptly declared himself for peace and disarmament.

In 1895, Carl Schurz suggested arbitration when a boundary dispute between Venezuela and British Guiana threatened to break out into armed conflict, not between those two states, but between England and the United States! This tense situation came about when Britain warned she would take action unless Venezuela settled the boundary on British terms. The United States Congress, of course, bristled at the threat of hemispheric invasion. President Cleveland cited the Monroe Doctrine and bluntly warned England that a thrust into the Western Hemisphere by a European power would be met by force.

Schurz had no illusions about war. He had already been through one revolution and a major conflict. He knew how impermanent military conquests could be, how permanent their scars. Neither did he stick his head in the sand. Schurz recognized the need for an adequate army and navy, and insisted it was the only way America could keep its standing in the world community. "But it must not, as our boyish jingoes wish it to do, swagger among the nations of the world with a chip on its shoulder, shaking its fists in everybody's face," he said in a speech before the New York Chamber of Commerce.

Schurz seldom offered criticism without a suitable remedy. He now outlined a bold plan to settle the Venezuelan argument: let an equal number of Americans and Englishmen form a commission. Let this group, under a neutral chairman, study the border in question, then submit their findings for arbitration.

Calm heads prevailed. Congress listened, Britain's Parliament considered, the Venezuelan government relented. The Schurz plan was agreed upon, and eventually a boundary line was settled to everyone's satisfaction.

With international peace as his newfound cause, Carl Schurz took to the public platform once again. "I have known war at its worst and I abhor it," he told the nation. "It should be only the very last resort even in contending for a just and beneficent end, after all the resources of peaceful methods have been exhausted. To me, arbitration is not only the most humane and economical method of settling international differences, but also the most, if not the only, certain method to furnish enduring results."

Carl's preoccupation with peace was momentarily interrupted by the presidential campaign of 1896, which again put heavy demands on his time and energy.

The Democrats had named William Jennings Bryan, an outspoken supporter of free silver—the unlimited coinage of silver at a ratio to gold of 16 to 1—as the basis for the nation's monetary system. His stand split Democratic ranks. Westerners and farmers favored free silver; sound money men, like Carl Schurz, insisted that any move away from gold would lead to disaster.

Running against Bryan was William McKinley, the conservative Republican, who based his campaign on a platform of "thrift, law, order and the full dinner pail."

Independents turned to Carl Schurz once again. Whom would he support?

It was a painful decision. On the one hand, Carl opposed McKinley for his high tariff policy. On the other, he could not support Bryan's silver program, which he termed "financial heresy."

He finally chose between what he felt to be the lesser of two evils. He backed McKinley; many independents followed him to the polls, though as reluctantly as he, and helped put the Republican conservative into office.

William McKinley knew that the editor was not a man to be ignored. Schurz had, after all, been closely associated, one way or another, with every President since 1860 with the exception of Harrison. Therefore, when the new Chief Executive came to New York early in 1897, Carl was one of his first invited callers.

He now seized the opportunity to warn McKinley about America's belligerent posture in international affairs. Cuba was then in rebellion against Spanish rule, and there was strong sentiment for American military intervention. But there was a question in Schurz's mind about the motives of those who wanted to send troops there. It seemed to him that such a move was prompted more by American sugar and fruit interests in Cuba than a desire to help the rebels in their fight for freedom.

He also warned against private interests then pushing for the annexation of the Hawaiian Islands. In addition, he reminded McKinley that there were rumors about acquiring the Spanish-held Philippine Islands. The proposed control of all these territories by the United States was lumped under the high-sounding slogan of America's "Manifest Destiny."

"Just another name for imperialism," Schurz said bluntly. "I urge you, sir, not to support an expansionist policy for the United States."

McKinley was a patient man. "Did you feel the same about the purchase of Alaska, Mr. Schurz? And was that not a valuable territorial acquisition for our nation?"

"It was, most certainly," Carl agreed. "If you go back into the records, sir, you will see that I supported that move editorially when everybody else was calling it Seward's Folly. There is this to be said for Alaska, and for the earlier expansion of our nation to Texas and California. All these lands are on the North American continent, not separated from Washington by hundreds, and in some cases thousands, of miles of ocean."

Schurz cited other objections: America would require a greatly expanded army and navy to control territories so far from home; he was also fearful of the spread of malaria and other tropical diseases. Furthermore, he doubted whether native populations would be adequately represented in Washington. "Above all," he concluded, "there is the very real danger of war if we jump pell-mell into the affairs of other nations, Spain in particular."

Perhaps Schurz was shortsighted in 1897. Perhaps he did not see the strategic value of the Philippines and Hawaii to the national defense. On the other hand, he recognized that private commercial interests at home would gain enormously if the United States held a strong hand in the Caribbean and Pacific areas.

Of course, Schurz had no way of knowing then that modern communications and advances in public health would have removed many of his objections. Also, the granting of political freedom to native populations on those islands was something he just could not predict in 1897.

At any rate, President McKinley assured his guest that "there will be no jingo nonsense under my administration. You need not borrow trouble on that account."

Schurz did not. After recording his interview in his private journal, he respectfully held his editorial tongue. But when, three months later, the President sent a treaty to the Senate calling for the annexation of Hawaii, Carl bitterly attacked the administration, and accused it of "serving a gang of sugar speculators in search of profit."

The fact that the Senate failed to approve the treaty that summer did not mollify Schurz. To him, the handwriting was on the wall. McKinley was obviously taking America along the path of her "Manifest Destiny."

That path became abundantly clear with the sinking of

the battleship *Maine* in the harbor of Havana, Cuba, on February 15, 1898. Two hundred and sixty American lives were lost. A shocked nation, led by the newspapers of William Randolph Hearst, called for immediate intervention. The cry of "Remember the *Maine!*" reverberated across the land. In a grimly determined mood, Congress appropriated an emergency fund to build up America's war machine.

Schurz called the tragedy a "ghastly mistake" in which both governments had to share the blame. He pointed out that an American battleship should never have been sent to a Spanish port while tensions were high between the two countries. The fact that Theodore Roosevelt was then the Assistant Secretary of the Navy only strengthened his belief that the United States, somehow, had invited the disaster. He filled his editorial columns with passionate pleas for arbitration. He even wrote personal letters to McKinley imploring him not to take any hasty action that would plunge the nation into war. He agreed that the Spanish government was needlessly slow in coming to terms or furnishing adequate explanations. "Even so," he wrote, "is it not better to wait and reason with one another than to rush into armed conflict from which there can be no safe return for hundreds, perhaps thousands, of lives?"

His lonely voice was drowned out by loud demands for "satisfaction" and for "action now to liberate the oppressed people of Cuba." Perhaps the loudest of these belonged to William Randolph Hearst, who mixed equal parts of patriotism and sensational journalism in his call for military action. Theodore Roosevelt, too, demanded that America shed its complacent ways and take up the "strenuous life" to protect its interests abroad.

Carl's answer was to draw up a series of peace resolutions

which he passed on to McKinley. "War at any price," these resolutions read, "is a price too high to pay."

He might as well have tried to capture the wind. Congress, in no mood to equivocate, declared war against Spain on April 25, 1898. It did so in spite of the fact that the Spanish government had called for an end of hostilities against the Cuban rebels eighteen days earlier and had even promised them limited home rule.

Schurz became one of the early casualties of the war. Realizing that he was hopelessly in the minority, and could no longer usefully serve the majority, he resigned from *Harper's*. "There seems to be little sentiment for peace," he confided to his daughters. "My species of journalism has suddenly become extinct. The flag-wavers and sword-rattlers have taken over our press."

Fortunately, he was no longer in need of a job. His payments for the early portions of his autobiography, and his fees from other published works, were sufficient for his needs.

Nor was he quite as alone in his opposition to war as he had first imagined. He found kindred souls in President Eliot of Harvard and Samuel Gompers, the labor leader. His constant friend and companion in his old age, Dr. Abraham Jacobi, also shared his passion for peace. Schurz gathered these and other like-minded men together in an effort to bring pressure on the administration.

But hardly had the peacemakers organized than the conflict came to a sudden end. After only four months of war, Spain sued for peace in August, 1898, following a series of crushing defeats led by "Rough Rider" Teddy Roosevelt on land and Admirals Schley and Dewey at sea.

Historians later called this a strange sort of war, marked by ineptitude on both sides. Spanish forces were hopelessly weak and their equipment outdated, while American armies were badly organized and poorly prepared for the tropics. Of the five thousand American fatalities in the Spanish-American War, less than five hundred died in battle. The rest succumbed to disease, bad food and the jungle.

But most Americans at the time cared little about statistics, or the fact that the toll might have been much higher had Spain had a first-rate military machine. The important thing was that America had gone to war with a foreign power and won. Equally important, she was about to reap the fruits of conquest—overseas territories!

This was all the challenge Carl Schurz needed to renew his energies. In a new flood of articles for independent magazines, he urged the United States to become a compassionate victor. "If America reaches out for colonies now," he warned in an open letter to President McKinley, "the world will be convinced that we went to war for selfish reasons, and not for the liberation of the oppressed."

McKinley said nothing. He didn't have to. Military power was king, and a new hero, Colonel Theodore Roosevelt, its crown prince.

The Treaty of Paris, signed in December, 1898, drew up terms of settlement between Spain and the United States. It ceded Puerto Rico, Guam and the Philippine Islands to the United States, the latter upon payment of $20 million. The treaty, however, had not yet gone into effect; it still had to be ratified by the Senate.

Colonial troubles for the victors broke out almost at once as bands of Filipinos rose up against their new masters in the Philippines. It took almost four years of jungle warfare to bring these dissident forces under control. Meantime, the passage of the Newlands Resolution in the summer of 1898 had finally made the Hawaiian Islands a territorial possession of the United States.

Carl Schurz denounced all these moves as expansionist actions, against the welfare of the native populations involved. His leadership won him election as vice president of the Anti-Imperialist League, made up of persons like himself who deplored America's newfound ambitions overseas. But aside from writing articles for the League and passing resolutions, his protests were as ineffective as grains of sand thrown into a roaring surf.

Still, they left their tracings on the record. When Theodore Roosevelt, still wearing his Rough Rider uniform, agreed to run for governor of New York under the Republican banner in 1898, he turned to his former civil service colleague and asked for his help. Carl firmly refused, citing his reasons in an open letter to the New York *Evening Post*. "Theodore Roosevelt," Schurz announced, "has an exceptionally bellicose temperament. I believe him to be dangerously deficient in that patient prudence which is necessary for the peaceable conduct of international relations. I also fear he is using the governorship of New York as a steppingstone to the Presidency."

Prophetic words, but the nation had eyes and ears only for the military leadership of Colonel Roosevelt. Though presumably running for state office, Roosevelt declared that "the first great principle of this nation is to uphold the national honor abroad." His audiences cheered, then swept him into office as governor of the most populous state of the Union. Obviously, Carl Schurz was still badly out of step.

Even so, he refused to give up. The Treaty of Paris had not yet been ratified. Until it had, anything could happen. If only he could carry his fight to the public more effectively!

Surprisingly, he found increasing support as the weeks passed. In January, 1899, he spoke at an international affairs forum sponsored by the University of Chicago. As an avowed anti-imperialist, he repeated his assertion that the recent war against Spain had been turned into "a land-grabbing game and an act of criminal aggression."

At least one man in the audience that night murmured approval. He, too, had a short white beard and deep furrows on either side of his ruddy face. His eyes were a pale blue, his gaze as keen and intent as the speaker's; his age, very close to the man addressing the forum; his name, Andrew Carnegie.

A person of exceptional wealth, Carnegie had amassed a fortune in steel, not always by the most ethical means. Following a long period of soul-searching and travel, he had turned over most of his wealth to education and world peace. He had come to Chicago to hear what Carl Schurz had to say about America's role in international affairs. What he heard apparently satisfied him greatly.

"History shows that military glory is the most unwholesome food that democracies can feed upon," Schurz continued as Carnegie nodded approval again. "We need not have any war today unless, without any compelling necessity, we choose to have it!"

After the meeting, Andrew Carnegie approached Carl Schurz. "You, sir," he said in his strong Scottish burr, "have the brains and I have the dollars. I can devote some of my dollars to spreading your brains."

14.

It was now a race against the calendar.

On one side were Schurz, Carnegie and the rest of the Anti-Imperialist League; on the other, the Treaty of Paris supporters, led by Senator Henry Cabot Lodge and John Hay, McKinley's Secretary of State. The finish line was at least a month off, at which time the Upper House was expected to vote on treaty ratification. The question was, who would get there first with the necessary number of votes?

The odds seemed to favor the McKinley forces. They had public opinion on their side, strong leadership and the Senate majority. However, the administration had to get the "advice and consent" of the Senate by at least a two-thirds margin in order to put the treaty into effect, as required by the Constitution. Lodge was certain he could round up enough votes, especially since a number of Democrats had already come out for ratification.

"Good!" Carl Schurz countered. "Sounds like Republican overconfidence. Maybe we'll catch them napping. If only we had more time!" His strategy was to rouse the public conscience in what little time remained. That done, perhaps enough senators could be persuaded to shift their positions.

The "brains and dollars" combination went into immediate action. With Carnegie's money, Schurz printed his anti-treaty talk as a pamphlet. Inside of a week, half a million copies were on their way to congressmen, editors, clergymen, educators, businessmen—anyone in a position to influence public opinion. Where newspapers would not report his pamphlet as news, Schurz bought advertising space in their pages. Where they refused to accept advertising, he printed handbills for local distribution.

The public conscience stirred. Fresh sentiment against the treaty reached Washington. If Senator Lodge thought he had clear sailing before the pamphlet attack, he certainly didn't think so by the end of that January. "It's this blasted broadside," he exploded to administration leaders, forgetting his Puritan gentility for the moment. "We've got a fight on our hands, make no mistake about it!"

Debate in the Senate was sharp, often acrimonious. Senators who had been thought to be safely on the side of ratification now began to express some doubts over America's expanding role in global affairs. Obviously, the antitreaty pamphlet was hitting its target.

Meanwhile, Schurz continued to apply pressure. "If the Philippines are so anxious to be protected by American laws and institutions as our treaty supporters claim," he thundered, "why are the Filipinos fighting American troops in the jungles and villages of the islands?" Why, indeed, citizens asked one another. Why, indeed, they asked their congressmen.

"The very least the administration can do," Schurz insisted in another public appeal, "is to hold off any decision on ratification until the national elections next year. I say let's make the Treaty of Paris an election issue, then let the voters decide."

Cabot Lodge anxiously measured the odds. His lead was dwindling rapidly. Time was now of the essence. All this negative talk had to stop and stop soon, or the administration might very well have a defeat on its hands instead of a victory.

Accordingly, a strategic rumor was "leaked" to newspaper reporters in Washington. It went something like this: everybody knew Germany was looking for colonies; what they didn't know, perhaps, was that she had already cast covetous eyes at the Philippines. Unless the Treaty of Paris won Senate approval in a matter of days, there was a very good chance that the former Spanish colonies would wind up under the Kaiser's flag!

"A hoax!" Schurz charged. "It's nothing but a McKinley smokescreen!"

Some people, however, weren't so sure. The State Department, they argued, should know what it was talking about. The rumor gathered momentum, picked up credibility. Why take a chance and let the Philippines slip out of American hands now? Besides, any new taxes as a result of protecting the islands would soon be made up by increased colonial trade, or so the stories went.

The administration's whispering campaign turned the tide. Opposition to the treaty diminished markedly. When the vote was finally taken on February 6, 1899, the Upper House approved the Treaty of Paris by the slim margin of a single vote. Henry Cabot Lodge heaved a sigh of relief.

"It was," he admitted to reporters after the vote, "the closest, hardest fight I have ever known." Close and hard, yes; but the United States Senate had officially given its "advice and consent" to America's expanding role in international affairs.

Wearily Schurz retreated from Washington, licking the wounds of his latest political defeat. With his seventieth birthday less than a month off, he felt tired, spent, discouraged. "There's no life left in this baggage of bones," he confessed to Dr. Abraham Jacobi upon his return to New York. "I might just as well go hide somewhere."

"Nonsense! Can't think of anything that would please Cabot Lodge more!"

"The senator from Massachusetts," Carl retorted, "is twenty years my junior. He can get off the floor after a hard fight. I can't."

"I see." Dr. Jacobi reached for his hat and coat. "By the way, Carl, how is your autobiography coming along?"

Schurz broke out into a chuckle. "You old soothsayer! You know just the right tonic for a patient like me, don't you?"

With that reminder, Carl returned to his autobiography with renewed determination. After all, he wasn't getting any younger. Time he picked up the thread of his life. His book had already progressed well into his career as editor-politician in the Midwest; he was now about to write his impressions of his first meeting with Abraham Lincoln.

"Now those were the years of happy struggle," he said to Agatha one night as they both sat working in the library of their New York apartment. "I wonder, does anyone remember them but me?"

She made light of his remarks. "Don't get sentimental, Father, or you'll be writing a novel instead of history."

"Perhaps I am getting a bit soft in my old age," he agreed. He pinched the pince-nez glasses off his nose, then brightened visibly. "Agatha, what do you say to a change of scene, eh? Perhaps a month or two in the South? New York winters chill me to the bone."

"Oh, no!" she burst out, too loudly.

"It's my bones! I should know—!"

Agatha quickly recovered herself. "I mean," she explained,

throwing a nervous glance at the calendar, "we shouldn't dream of traveling now, not while the manuscript is going so well." A date on that calendar had been fixed in her mind —March 2, 1899, her father's seventieth birthday, now less than a week away. She and Dr. Jacobi and Gustav Schwab had made great plans for that day. Nothing, not even a trip South, must interfere with it. "We'll think about a vacation later, after you complete this chapter on Lincoln."

Carl sighed and replaced his glasses. "I suppose you're right, Agatha. You usually are." He turned to gaze at a framed photograph of his late wife. "Just like your mother."

"Lincoln!" she commanded, tapping her notebook. "Shall I read from your diary?"

They continued working until nearly midnight. When her father finally went off to bed, Agatha Schurz opened a locked desk drawer, took out a long list of names, then checked them off against another list. Everyone to whom she and Marianne had written—the birthday committee had agreed on four hundred names—had said they would be proud and happy to be present at a testimonial dinner on the evening of March 2, in honor of Carl Schurz's seventieth birthday.

Agatha leaned back in her chair, smiling happily. Now if she could only keep the secret from him for just a few more days!

"Go out on a night like this? It's raining cats and dogs!" Carl glanced out the window of his bedroom. "And in formal clothes, too! Whatever for?"

"For a benefit affair, Father!" Just like him to offer resistance right up until the last moment, she thought. Here it was an hour before the party and he was still fussing with his clothes.

"Why can't we eat at home?" Carl asked again, perhaps for the tenth time that day. "You know dining out gives me heartburn!"

"Not at Delmonico's, Father!"

"Then it'll burn a hole in my wallet. Couldn't we go to a less expensive place?"

Agatha lifted her eyes in exasperation. She was almost on the verge of giving away the entire plot. "Hurry along now. We mustn't keep the cab waiting."

"Stuff and nonsense," Schurz grumbled, slipping into a dress shirt. Then, "Confound it, Agatha!" he roared. "Come and help me with these cuff links!"

Father and daughter finally arrived at Delmonico's with the grumpy Schurz none the wiser. She had told him they would have a quiet dinner, then hurry off to the "benefit affair."

He was still mumbling and grumbling as she pushed him gently through the great front doors of the restaurant. Only then, when he heard the band and the cheers and saw the bright lights and the gaily bedecked tables did Carl Schurz realize he had been led into a trap.

"Happy birthday, Carl!"

The chorus of good wishes from four hundred guests descended on him like thunder. Schurz had faced any number of situations in his life. He had stood before kings and presidents, before cannon and charging horses, before political opponents and irate hecklers. He had flinched before none of them. But now he fell back, taken completely by surprise.

"Happy birthday, old friend!" Coming at him with outstretched hands were Gustav Schwab, Dr. Jacobi and Andrew Carnegie. The three elderly gentlemen escorted the dumbfounded Schurz to his seat of honor while the band played merrily on and the guests cheered. Waiting at the head table were Marianne and his sons, Carl, Jr., and Herbert.

"Happy birthday, Father!" they laughed.

Few events in his life moved Schurz as much as the party tendered him that night. Flanked by his family and surrounded by hundreds of his close friends and associates, he sat through the long dinner, nodding and blinking and smiling. For once, he could think of little to say except to mutter a gruff "Benefit affair, indeed!"

After dinner came coffee, cigars and speeches, with Gustav Schwab acting as toastmaster. The financier got the ceremonies off to an impressive start by announcing that a fund was being raised to start a Carl Schurz Memorial Library at Columbia University and to endow a Schurz Chair of Literature at that institution. "And to show that we here, ourselves, are not lacking in the rhetoric for which our guest of honor is distinguished," he continued, "I will propose a series of toasts to milestones in his career, with brief responses by those who know him best. My first toast, ladies and gentlemen: To Carl Schurz and his days of storm and stress in the Germany of his youth."

Glasses were lifted as Dr. Abraham Jacobi rose to his feet. With simple but sincere words, he reviewed Carl's days at the University of Bonn, including the incredible rescue of Gottfried Kinkel. The assembled guests cheered.

Toastmaster Schwab raised his glass again. "To Carl Schurz, champion of the slave!" The response came from Professor William Sloane, of Princeton, a leading historian, who traced Carl's early career in America, especially his uncompromising stand against slavery.

"To Carl Schurz, soldier in the Civil War!" Schwab went on. The response this time came from John Lockman, the military historian.

The next toast was to "Carl Schurz, Senator of the United States." This part of his career was covered by Moorfield Storey, another close friend and associate.

There were also toasts to Carl's role as a cabinet member, Mugwump leader and political editor. But the biggest cheer of all was reserved for Schwab's salute to "Carl Schurz, the advocate of civil service!" Appropriately, this phase was covered by Edward Shepherd, himself an author, civil service reformer and public servant.

When finally it came time for the guest of honor to speak, he could find no words to express himself. Rising slowly to his feet, he looked out at a sea of faces; a misty blur ran them all together. "My dear . . . my very dear friends," Carl managed at last, "you have paid me honors that should be reserved for a far more worthy individual." Then regaining control, he added with a smile, "I could hardly recognize the individual so glowingly described tonight by such kind and indulgent friends. Yes, indulgent, since errors dot my past like sparrows on telegraph wires. True, true," he admitted as denials were raised. "For a man not to have made mistakes in his lifetime means that he has either been asleep or indifferent during all those years. I hope I have been neither. But whatever the result of my past actions, whether with or without error, I can tell you that I have never said or done anything in my adult life that I did not believe to be true and honest!"

The answering cheers were deafening. Carl Schurz remained standing, nodding and smiling at the ovation. Then, overcome by emotion, he slumped to his chair, took off his glasses and wiped his eyes unashamedly.

He was honored again later that year by Columbia University, which conferred on him an honorary degree of Doctor of Laws in June, 1899. The commencement citation saluted him as "a man who, for more than half a century and in two hemispheres, has been making law, not in one or two ways, but in all the ways in which law is made. He has written and spoken and fought, in the old world and the new, for the great causes of our century. What his youth longed for, his age has seen fulfilled."

After the campus ceremonies, Carl Schurz and Dr. Jacobi traveled to their summer retreat at Lake George. As the train puffed along the peaceful Hudson River Valley, Jacobi turned to his friend. "What his youth longed for, his age has seen fulfilled," he repeated softly. Then he playfully nudged him. "Still feel like an old baggage of bones, Carl?"

Schurz grinned happily. "Yes, Abraham. But maybe now, not so useless."

In the lives of all men shadows fall where sunshine played a moment before. So it was with Carl Schurz, as mortal as any man.

On the return trip home from Lake George, he fell desperately ill on the train. His vision jumped, his heart beat faded, his skin felt hot and dry. Shafts of pain cut through his feverish brow.

Luckily, Dr. Jacobi had insisted on going with him. His friend had seemed somewhat under the weather that morning; this attack, whatever it was, supported the doctor's suspicions. "Only a little longer," he whispered. "We'll be home in an hour."

Jacobi took Carl to his own home and put him to bed at once where a more careful examination confirmed his earlier diagnosis: the patient had an acute attack of ptomaine poisoning. For the next few days, Carl's life hung in the balance. Then his will to live, as much as his strong heart, pulled him through. After the crisis had passed, he smiled wanly at Dr.

Jacobi. "You . . . you didn't think I'd leave you now, before the turn of the century, did you, Abraham?" he whispered weakly. "We're supposed to share a bottle of champagne when 1900 comes around, remember?"

"I remember." Jacobi reached for his brow. He found it cool and damp. "How do you feel, old friend?"

Carl closed his eyes. "Tired . . . baggage of bones . . . useless!"

"Of course you're tired," Jacobi agreed. "You've been through the fight of your life."

But Carl heard nothing. He was already fast asleep, storing up energy for the next crisis in his life.

It came sooner than anyone had a right to expect. He had hardly regained his health when a cable arrived from England where Herbert had gone for an extended vacation after graduating from Harvard. Agatha read it first, then, after calling in Dr. Jacobi, showed it to her father.

"Regret to inform you," Carl read, the cable quivering in his hands, "of the death of Herbert Schurz, your son, due to coronary failure. Please advise disposition of the body." The terse message was signed by a London physician.

The elder Schurz gripped his cane. "Agatha, pack my bags!"

Dr. Jacobi moved between father and daughter. "You're in no condition to travel now, Carl. If you insist on going after Herbert, there will be two bodies to bring back. I suggest you send someone else."

Schurz fell back into a chair. His hair was whiter now, the stoop of his shoulders more pronounced; his voice had lost much of its old fire. "What did I tell you, Abraham? I'm useless!" He shook his head. "Useless!" he whispered again.

15.

"Happy New Year, Carl!"

"Happy New *Century,* Abraham!" Carl waved his cigar in the general direction of the window. "Let's hope the new one begins a good deal better than the old one ended."

Outside, a cacophony of bells, whistles and horns paid noisy tribute to the year 1900. The fact that a new century was dawning seemed to add a note of urgency to the celebration. But Carl Schurz felt curiously detached from everything, even from the gay little family party going on in the next room. After having wished his daughters and son and a few old friends a subdued New Year's greeting, he had gone back to his study for a few quiet words with Dr. Jacobi. He listened a moment more to the sounds of revelry, let out a deep sigh, then sank into a deep chair.

The doctor decided against forcing a note of cheer. After all, it *had* been a difficult year for his old friend. First, that illness last summer which had almost cost him his life. Then the death of his son; that had really affected him.

"I'm going back with the young folk," Jacobi finally said. "Here in the darkness, I look too much like Father Time."

Carl managed a wry smile at the little joke. Sitting alone, in the dimness of the study, he came to the bitter-sweet conclusion that he was getting old. He hardly needed the reminder of the years to tell him that. The ever diminishing ranks of old friends and colleagues were silent testimony to his own advancing yars. The names and faces of the dead seemed to be carried in by the pealing of the midnight bells . . . Charles Sumner, Horace Greeley, Rutherford Hayes, Charles Francis Adams, George William Curtis, Francis Grund, Gottfried Kinkel . . .

A familiar voice roused him from his revery. "And why so pensive at such a happy time?"

Carl opened his eyes with a start. His daughter Marianne, smiling prettily, was holding out her hand. "You may have the honor, sir, of the first dance of the new century with your obedient servant." She made a little curtsy in front of him.

He got slowly to his feet. "Dear lady," he answered with playful formality, "nothing would give me greater pleasure." He gave her his arm and escorted her to the next room. Now this is more like it, he said to himself, leading her in a stately waltz. A man can think about the past only so long.

"Happy New Year, Carl!" One of his guests, an editor from the old days, waved at him over Marianne's shoulder. "What do you think of McKinley's chances for re-election this year, eh?"

Schurz scowled. What could ever be happy about a year that was certain to see the McKinley administration back in power?

Carl's heart was hardly in the campaign of 1900. McKinley and William Jennings Bryan were going at it again, offering the nation the same dreary choice—high tariffs and expansionism as against free silver. On the theory that anything was better than the administration's aggressive policies, Schurz voted for Bryan and glumly saw him go down to defeat for the second time. Worse from his point of view, the Vice Presidency that year went to Theodore Roosevelt, still riding high on his war record, still rattling his sword.

In a bitter and angry mood he penned a letter to the *Evening Post*. "There is a very widespread feeling," he announced, "that the people have permitted themeslves to be forced by two rotten old party carcasses to choose between two evils." In other words, a plague on both your houses! If ever there was a time for Schurz to quit politics, this was it, his friends said to one another.

But they did not count on history or Carl's almost involuntary reflexes to a demanding political situation, even at the age of seventy-one.

The stage was set by another of those brutal acts of violence which have marred America's history. In the summer of 1901, an assassin took the life of William McKinley. Carl deplored the tragedy, though he had no love for the late President's policies. It seemed incredible that three Chief Executives had been cut down in the prime of life and office, all within his active career! Almost as hard to believe was the fact that the man with whom he had waged a desperate fight on foreign affairs was now in the White House!

Theodore Roosevelt was sworn into office on September 14, 1901, the day McKinley died. At the age of forty-two, he was the youngest man ever to hold that high office.

From the beginning, Schurz made it clear that he would support the new President if the latter followed what he called "right principles and methods." To Carl, this meant caution in foreign affairs, autonomy for the Philippines and a reasonable approach to disarmament.

He had little to complain about during Roosevelt's first year in office. In fact, he was delighted with the administration's moves on the domestic scene. Schurz was in agreement with Roosevelt's trust-busting and applauded his insistence on a fair labor policy, long overdue. Of course, he backed his conservation measures all the way. And when Roosevelt sent a message to Congress calling for a cabinet post for commerce and labor, Schurz sent him a warm note of approval.

But when the President dropped the other political shoe, when he revealed his foreign policy, Schurz and he parted company. Far from granting autonomy to the Philippines, Roosevelt clamped an even tighter control on the islands. He continued his aggressive pose by sending his navy out on the high seas as evidence of America's might and right. Carl felt that the risks which the President was taking in the conduct of foreign affairs far outweighed his domestic policies, admirable as those were.

He and Andrew Carnegie joined forces once again. Together they pleaded with Roosevelt to moderate his foreign policy. The President listened politely but promised nothing. In his personal letters, he referred to men like Schurz and Carnegie and President Eliot of Harvard as "professional peace advocates." Publicly, he said that he placed peace as "second to righteousness."

This was too much for Schurz. "I am old and sometimes tired," he confessed toward the end of 1902, "but this is a great and solemn crisis. I cannot remove myself from the complex of current affairs."

That crisis reached a shrill pitch in 1903 when Colombia refused to sign a treaty with the United States giving the latter the right to lease land on the Isthmus of Panama for the purposes of building a canal linking the Atlantic and Pacific Oceans. The area, or department, of Panama was then a part of Colombia.

A few months later, Panama revolted against her mother country. When President Roosevelt dispatched a cruiser to the waters off the Isthmus, Schurz was certain that the administration was headed for disaster. There were charges then, as later, that the President had deliberately encouraged the Panamanian revolt in order to effect the treaty spurned earlier by Colombia. His critics, including Schurz, had no quarrel about building the "Big Ditch." But they strongly objected to the manner by which the United States had taken possession of the Canal Zone. Roosevelt's later boast that "I took Panama," while supposedly spoken in jest, only confirmed the suspicions of his critics.

To Schurz's vast relief, nothing unpleasant came of the Canal Zone incident, which culminated in the Hay-Bunau-Varilla Treaty of November, 1903.

When Theodore Roosevelt won Republican renomination in 1904, he chose two of his most influential spokesmen, John Hay, his Secretary of State, and Elihu Root, his Secretary of War, to present the administration's campaign promises to the American public. Together, they did a masterful job.

The Democrats, who had nominated Judge Alton B. Parker as their presidential candidate, searched desperately for someone with enough prestige to answer them. They could find no one better qualified than Carl Schurz, then seventy-five years old.

Judge Parker, a man of great dignity and formality, sent Schurz a personal appeal. "It is of the first importance that our opponents be answered by a man of intellectual strength, character and position. Since no one fills that requirement so well, I make bold to ask you to do it."

Carl read the letter several times in the privacy of his study. Then he took off his glasses, blew his nose into an enormous handkerchief and settled back with a satisfied sigh. He was far from through!

But he hadn't counted on Dr. Jacobi. "Out of the question, Carl! You'll never survive the rigors of the campaign trail. Leave that to younger, more active men. But there's no reason why you can't give Parker the benefit of your mind . . . from the comfort of your study. See if the party will be satisfied with an article or a pamphlet. . . . No!" he warded off his friend's protests. "Personal appearances are out of the question!"

The party had to settle for the message instead of the man. In a lengthy article which he wrote for the nation's press, Carl Schurz compared the platforms and candidates—the Republicans' against the Democrats', Roosevelt against Parker. As a political tract, it was frankly partisan. As a personality portrait of the two men, it was a *tour de force*.

Schurz presented Judge Parker as a dignified, cultured and wise humanitarian, a candidate who relied on logic rather than bluster, reason in place of threats, firmness instead of rigidity—very nearly the man Parker actually was.

But in describing Roosevelt, Carl was merciless, using some of the personality techniques of Sigmund Freud whose writings were just coming into prominence at the time. "There are two Roosevelts," Schurz explained. "The ideal, the legendary Roosevelt as he once appeared, and as many people still imagine him to be; and the real Roosevelt as he has since developed. His temperament is altogether too strong for his reason."

He also used irony with devastating effect. "President Roosevelt is an exceedingly interesting, picturesque and forcible character," he wrote, "who would have found a most congenial field of action at the time of the Crusades. But sometimes, he strangely fails to appreciate the higher moral aims of modern civilization."

The electorate, however, did not share Schurz's insight. They went all out for the "ideal, the legendary Roosevelt";

they delighted in his robust strength, his "common man" approach to democracy, his blunt language that defied big business at home and big powers abroad. Alton B. Parker never had a chance in the elections of 1904. Thus Schurz ended his long political career backing a loser.

In retrospect, his record for picking presidential winners was hardly a poor one. Of the twelve national elections in which Schurz voted, he backed eight winners and four losers —Greeley in 1872, Cleveland in 1888, Bryan in 1900 and Parker in 1904. Equally interesting, he voted six times for a Republican, six times for a Democrat.

Perhaps his greatest contribution to American politics was his firm belief that it was more important to vote for principle rather than party. He gave his time, his energy, his considerable talents as a writer and orator, to whatever party or organization promised most to the cause of good government.

Carl Schurz's public appearances after the 1904 campaign were few. Forbidden by his physician to exert himself—he was constantly troubled by a bronchial condition in his later years—he fulfilled only the most urgent engagements. In June, 1905, he traveled to the University of Wisconsin, which awarded him an honorary Doctor of Laws degree. A few months later, he spoke at a Negro rights rally in Chicago at Andrew Carnegie's request. But for the most part, he remained at home—in his New York apartment in the winter, at Pocantico Hills or Lake George in the summer—working on his autobiography, which he finally decided to call *Reminiscences.* He worked slowly, carefully, like someone unraveling a tangled web that holds within its strands more than a half century of political activity in which he himself, in company with Presidents, cabinet secretaries, congressmen, educators, lawyers, editors, businessmen, writers, musicians and philosophers, played such an important part.

It was Carl's habit, in these later years, to work on his autobiography in the mornings, then, after a light lunch, go to his favorite club in midtown Manhattan for a chat or a game of chess with one or another of his old friends. He was about to leave his apartment one brisk November day in 1905, when Agatha gently reminded him to take his umbrella. "Looks like rain, Father. Better take this."

"It's only a block to the streetcar—"

"And don't forget to wear your rubbers. We'll have no coughs and colds this winter." She tucked the muffler securely into the opening of his overcoat.

"All right, all right!" But his mutters and mumbles were more to maintain his parental dignity than to protest his daughter's watchful concern over his health. "You'd think I didn't know right from rain. Humph!"

He kissed her good-bye, then walked a short block to Madison Avenue, nodding to shopkeepers and passersby along the way. When he boarded the streetcar, the conductor collected his fare with a cordial greeting. Carl Schurz was as well known to the common folk of his neighborhood as he was to the political elite.

He made his way to the sunny side of the car and sat down. Twenty minutes later, the conductor gently prodded him. "Your stop next, Mr. Schurz."

Carl shook himself awake. "Dozing again," he muttered. He got up stiffly and made for the rear exit. "Must be careful, or one of these days you'll sleep clear down to—"

"Look out, Mr. Schurz!"

The warning came too late. Still somewhat stiff from his nap, Carl missed his footing and tumbled down the two steps of the street car. As he fell heavily on to the cobblestones, a shock of pain roared through his body. Then a blanket of darkness engulfed him.

"A broken hip," Dr. Jacobi told him next morning. "Not the easiest thing in the world to heal, especially at your age, Carl. But it will, if you follow my directions."

Schurz made a sour face. "Do I have any choice?"

A month later, he was on his way south, with Agatha constantly at his side. The hip was healing well, much to Jacobi's satisfaction. By next April, with the cast removed, Carl could hobble around well enough with the aid of a cane. "As good as new," he chuckled. "Let's go back to New York soon, Agatha. I miss the city and my old friends. Besides, we have much more work to do on my autobiography . . . so much more."

He never wrote another word of it. No sooner did he return to New York than he contracted pneumonia, the enemy of old age. He fought off the illness for days, his brave old heart continuing to beat. But then on May 14, 1906, he began to fail quickly. Feeling perhaps that the end was near, he motioned his children closer to his bedside. Carl, Jr., Marianne and Agatha bent over his spent body.

Schurz tried to speak; his lips moved soundlessly, gasping for breath. Then, with a final effort and a suggestion of a smile, he managed a hoarse whisper. "It is so simple . . . to die."

Those were his last words. Fittingly enough, they were spoken in German.

Like his entire life, Carl Schurz's funeral was simple and without pretention. And like his life, it touched a great many people, all of whom mourned the passing of a man who asked so little for himself, so much for others. Theodore

Roosevelt and Grover Cleveland sent condolences; Mark Twain wept at his funeral; his pallbearers were men of the highest distinction: Gustav Schwab, the financier; Dr. Abraham Jacobi, his closest friend and constant companion; Oscar S. Straus, the prominent merchant; Joseph Choate, the educator; Andrew Carnegie, his embattled fellow reformer and philanthropist, and Charles Francis Adams, Jr., grandson of the President.

He was eulogized by presidents of three great educational institutions, Hampton Institute, Tuskegee and Harvard. A memorial service in his honor packed Carnegie Hall, while the New York Symphony Orchestra played the music he knew and loved so well, but had so little time to enjoy in his long and busy lifetime.

A great high school in Chicago now bears his name. So does a tiny park in New York City, not far from where he lived; it affords a quiet oasis in a noisy, throbbing metropolis. An appropriate monument to Carl Schurz as Germany's "Great Son" stands at his birthplace in Liblar. A simple grave marks his burial place in Sleepy Hollow Cemetery in Tarrytown, New York, near his beloved Pocantico Hills.

But perhaps his most impressive memorial is a nine-foot-high bronze statue on Morningside Heights, on the campus of Columbia University in New York. Two massive stone benches on either side of the statue are marked by bronze bas-relief figures; one symbolizes the American Indian, the other, the American Negro. On the pedestal of the statue itself are inscribed these words: "Carl Schurz, Defender of Liberty and Friend of Human Right."

BIBLIOGRAPHY

Birnie, Arthur, *The Economic History of Europe*. Dial Press, 1930.

Catton, Bruce, *The Coming Fury*. Doubleday & Company, Inc., 1961.

Easum, Chester V., *The Americanization of Carl Schurz*. University of Chicago Press, 1929.

Fast, Howard M., *The Last Frontier*. Duell, Sloan & Pearce, 1941.

Fuess, Claude Moore, *Carl Schurz, Reformer*. Dodd, Mead & Company, 1932.

Handlin, Oscar, *The Uprooted*. Little, Brown & Co., 1951.

Miers, Earl Schenck, ed., *The American Story*. Channel Press, 1956.

Morison, Samuel Eliot & Commager, Henry Steele, *The Growth of the American Republic*, rev. ed. 2 vols. Oxford University Press, 1951.

Schurz, Carl, *The Autobiography of Carl Schurz*. (Abridged). Charles Scribner's Sons, 1961.

Schurz, Carl, *Intimate Letters*, trans. and ed. by Joseph Schafer. State Historical Soc. of Wisconsin, 1928.

New York Times. *America's Taste*. Simon and Schuster, 1960.

Reference Works: *Encyclopaedia Britannica;* Enc. Brit. Inc., 1955

Dictionary of American History; Scribner, 1940

Dictionary of American Biography; Scribner, 1943

Columbia Encyclopedia; Columbia University Press, 1958

Encyclopedia of American History; Harper, 1953.

Index